T0065285

No-Nonsense Life Skills

MANAGING YOUR STRESS

Dr. Ray Ashurst, Ph.D.

WESTBOW
PRESS®
A DIVISION OF THOMAS NELSON
& ZONDERVAN

WestBow Press books may be ordered through booksellers or by contacting:

WestBow Press
A Division of Thomas Nelson & Zondervan
1663 Liberty Drive
Bloomington, IN 47403
www.westbowpress.com
1 (866) 928-1240

ISBN: 978-1-5127-0770-0 (sc)
ISBN: 978-1-5127-0772-4 (hc)
ISBN: 978-1-5127-0771-7 (e)

Print information available on the last page.

WestBow Press rev. date: 01/12/2016

CONTENTS

ACKNOWLEDGEMENTS

The phenomenal cover of this book was created
by a genius of photography, *Chris Hefferen*.
If you were drawn to the cover, the credit
entirely belongs to him.

Throughout the stages of writing this book,
I was indeed fortunate to have proofreaders who
were not only friends but literary cheerleaders:
Carolyn Baker
Ed Durben
Doris Durben

Putting together the "extras" that are included
in the sale of this book required tedious work,
and I have three people to thank:
Carolyn Baker
Amy Grice
Opal Young

My anxiety over writing this first book was calmed
Down by *Ms. Grace Stevens* at WestBow Publishers.

INTRODUCTION

There are dozens and dozens of self-help books on the market, discussing every conceivable subject matter. I know that this book is not destined to literary immortality, like Harper Lee's book, **To Kill A Mockingbird**. What I do know about this book is that its contents changed my life in a dynamic, spiritual way. There is absolutely no nonsense about any of the Life Skills in this book. I am living proof that they work. That is not to say that once learned, once mastered. The Skills must be faced head-on every single day. They require a person to make a personal commitment to use these Skills in one's relationship to self and to others. I hope that they will mean as much to you as they have to me.

Our lives do not have to be horrible, depressing, and manic. Such a type of life changed for me on one cool, December evening, in 1982, on the dock of my parents' Florida home. I had reached my wit's end. Staring into the soothing water, I became convicted by God to seek some type of help regarding my conflicts. So, at the age of 38, I began a journey that transformed me and my way of life. The concepts in this book were responsible for the renewing of my mind and spirit.

Why such a book after all these years? Not to acquire wealth, for sure. Not even for recognition. Simply because God convicted me that it was time. I can truthfully say that His thoughts have guided me through these pages. Such a statement does not intend at all to portray me as a super Christian hero. I am not. I am simply a traveler as you are on this unpredictable journey in life.

Not everyone who begins reading this book may have any spiritual relationship with God. This book is not designed to evaluate or to diagnose your relationship with God. It is meant for all individuals to be able to appreciate, to understand, and to apply the ideas found within. It might challenge you in a certain way to be actively involved in a spiritual journey of your own. That is entirely up to you. One thing is for certain. The messages in **No-Nonsense Life Skills** can create changes in your life that will lead you to have quite an exhilarating life journey and adventure.

You may not agree with the total book. That's okay. You might just pick up some points throughout the book that will transform your life into an abundant one. *Good luck, happy reading, and enjoy the journey.*

****

You are always only one choice
away from changing your life.

---Marcy Blochowiak

****

Always, Always, Remember...

We are not humans having a spiritual
experience. We are spiritual beings
having a human experience.

--*Pierre Teilhard de Chardin*

****

CHAPTER 1

NO-NONSENSE SANDBOX

Go confidently in the direction of your dreams. Live the life you have imagined.

--Henry David Thoreau

Dedicated to Dr. Jarle Brors and Dr. Jay Craig, my therapists who taught me many life lessons.

--Vacation MT--E-1

CHAPTER 1

We are all familiar with the standard sandbox. Most of us grew up with one in our backyard. In it we had our toys and what-nots, and they usually stayed in it... most of the time. After we finished playing for the day, we were supposed to return everything into our box so that it would be prepared for the next day.

On a different level, the sandbox represents our personal space. Throughout the years we have been in someone's space, accidentally or purposefully. And on the flip side of the coin, some folks have been in ours. We had that uncomfortable feeling when someone was in our space (or sandbox). We felt as if the air was being sucked out of us, mainly due to our not asking that person to be in it. Picture the sandbox as your personal space.

When anyone gets too close to us in our space, it is as though that individual has trespassed into our imaginary sandbox. We didn't ask the persons to enter, but alas! The individuals are there. They may believe that we need our lives straightened out, and the uninvited guests have decided that it is their mission in life to enter uninvited into our sandbox to become our mentor.

In our sandbox, we have our symbolic possessions: our dreams, future plans, our family, our friends, and much more. Our comfortable sandbox is filled with every single thing we treasure. It is our world, all contained in a tiny space...our sandbox. It includes every facet of who we are, who we used to be, and what we would like to become. Thus, we are very protective of our sandbox and who is allowed in it.

The conflict arises when people enter into our space (sandbox) who were never invited. There are those folks who are not given an invitation, but they brazenly intrude in our space—our personal, valuable sandbox. They proceed immediately to instruct us on how we should manage our lives and our relationships. It is amazing how others believe they know how to manage our lives much better than we do.

It should not come as a big shock that some individuals in our arena firmly believe that they know how we should best conduct our life, with whom, and where. The ideals, hopes, and dreams in our sandbox get tossed out—the very things that made us today who we are. The sad story is that some of these people also believe that God is guiding them to conduct such behavior in our sandbox. And count on this: many of these unwelcome individuals live their own lives in quiet desperation.

Make no mistake. There are those who will challenge and question God about how He is actually working in our personal lives. If it differs from what they think is best for us, then God takes second place to them.

While in our sandbox, some individuals will attempt to wreak havoc in it. They may claim that God is telling them to be in our space and that God has spoken to them on our behalf. This is how it works: the acquaintance wanders into our sandbox and figuratively tosses out every single thing that individual finds unacceptable—we may have certain spiritual beliefs and values in which that acquaintance may not agree. Then according to this uninvited guest, we need to change our value system. But wait! The individual doesn't stop there. Your values, belief system, and spiritual convictions will all be severely questioned, examined, and evaluated. Tossing out some of your values from your sandbox can be an exciting challenge for this unwanted guest. And it doesn't stop there: next come your relationships. Certain relationships will not be tolerated, and according to your invading visitor, these relationships should end.

Everything in our sandbox will be judged. Here is the kicker: after creating havoc in our sandbox, the individuals will depart with a satisfied look of victory. When we then have the time to examine what is left in our sandbox, very little is there that we once treasured and revered. Our sandbox looks as if a hurricane has ripped it apart.

We try to re-establish our lives and re-construct our sandbox—the values, spiritual beliefs, material possessions, and relationships. This task requires a humongous amount of time and energy. We try desperately to re-supply our sandbox, and we attempt to make sense of what has occurred. Our sandbox is a disaster.

As soon as we believe that we have our lives in some order again, knocking at our door is another person wandering into our sacred space—uninvited. And here we go again, around the mulberry bush. A similar experience takes place, and we find ourselves trying to rescue our values, beliefs, material possessions, and relationships all over again. Very tiring! These uninvited invasions into our sandbox can happen over, over, and over. Keeping our sanity seems impossible.

****

The healthy, strong individual is the one wholeheartedly asks for help when he needs it, whether he has an abscess of his knee or in his soul.

--Rona Barrett

****

At 38 years old, I was continually allowing everyone and I mean, everyone, to infiltrate my space (sandbox). My sandbox remained in turmoil. I was miserable and because I was a "people-pleaser" I hobbled through my life allowing people to enter my sandbox, uninvited. Up to that time, I had never learned to stand up for myself, and I suffered terribly.

While visiting my parents one year at Christmas, I stood alone on their dock one beautiful evening. I remember praying aloud, *"God, I need your help. I'm so tired and frustrated living like this. Please help me."* While watching the wake hit the dock by the nightly passing boats, the answer from God was as clear as a beautiful, sunny, spring day in the Georgia mountains. His message: *"I have not abandoned you. I've been waiting on you. When you return home, I promise to guide you to someone who will help you."* I remembered the verse: *"I will never leave thee, nor forsake thee."* (Hebrews 13:5)

Protecting the privacy of one's sandbox is a daily task. You and I cannot risk being caught off our guard. There will be individuals who will definitely show up in our sandbox—uninvited! Some will appear every single day to evaluate, to re-organize, and to change the contents in our lives. Out may go our value system, beliefs, dreams, and goals. And we allow it! Some of us have permitted it since an early age, so as adults we stand by helpless, hopeless, and angry as our sandbox is mutilated.

The question we must ask is, *"Did we invite the individual into our space or did that person enter our sandbox uninvited?"*

How do we put an end to all the uninvited guests in our sandbox? **Warning**: If you decide to put an end to the uninvited sandbox intruders, people's feelings are going to be placed on the chopping block. These unwelcome individuals who charge into another person's sandbox in order to offer their pearls of wisdom must be confronted. Hang on because this part of your journey can become rough.

The real issue boils down to whether we wish to take control of our life. There will be times when we need to invite someone into our sandbox. It is a genuine request. All of us need to vent, to examine issues, and to seek guidance. We have certainly been at times at our wit's end, and at those moments we need the input from those whom we trust. There are also times when we just need to get issues off our chests but not necessarily needing any advice, suggestions, or direction. Therefore, we must establish our boundaries with those particular invited guests: they need to know when it is venting time or when it is desperate-for-advice time. But, we are to make the situation clear of what we expect when we have someone visit our sandbox. It is not their decision to establish the boundaries. After all, it is our sandbox! Sometimes it is difficult to find someone who will just listen, but keep searching, God is faithful to provide you with the right person at the right moment.

****

We wonder why it is that well-meant advice and constructive criticism, like a hat someone else has put on your head, never feels just right.

--Eleasnor Doan

****

Again, the times we invite an individual into our sandbox with the expressed idea to simply vent, need to be spelled out at the very beginning: *"I need to get things off my chest, and I just need someone to listen. No feedback, advice, or suggestions. Just listen."* Even if the persons are good friends, we still must establish our boundaries—please just listen or offer some suggestions when I ask.

We all have certain folks in our lives who think they have the market on wisdom and on experience. And they are just itching to take over our sandbox as theirs. Some may be relatives, neighbors, or shopping buddies. At the precise moment we are about to be verbally bombarded by the rhetoric of our uninvited guest, we have to make a rapid decision: *"Do we allow this person to remain uninvited in our sandbox, creating havoc, or do we ask the individual to politely vacate...and be sure to bundle up in case it's cold outside."* This is the point when bruised feelings may occur.

Such action of ours can seem devastating at the time. After all, we may not be accustomed to being so bold. We may, at first, feel very weird, maybe extremely uncomfortable. Offended feelings can certainly take place. In their minds, *"How dare you give me such an ultimatum of remaining silent or of leaving. After all, I may have all the solutions to your problems. This is the thanks I get for all that I have done for you?"*

Our personal feelings and thoughts may be tender because of the ultimatum we just presented. We may question whether we want unsolicited advice or not? What is the right thing to do? Am I being a horrible person for setting forth such boundaries? So, on top of what issues are already perplexing us, now our sandbox may have a litter odor of uninvited advice. Don't worry about your dilemma because the more you set your perimeters, the more comfortable you become with them. If you can locate someone in your personal arena who is comfortable just listening (without the need of advice-giving), then hang on to that person with all your strength and might—they are a rare species and as good as gold.

It's no embarrassment that we need someone to talk with at times. All of us have conflicts. The mountains are not going to shake, the rivers are not going to dry up, and life will continue. Everyone needs a true-blue friend who will accept us unconditionally...and listen to us when we need it.

"A friend loveth at all times." – Proverbs 17:17

In eternity past, God knew that we would need special people in our lives to assist us through the perils and disasters in life. God is not going to be shocked or surprised when we finally get to the point of being real, truthful, and genuine with our thoughts, actions, and feelings. Therefore, when you need to seek help, then invite that special person into your sandbox. But, be fair. Again, your guest should be informed at the onset of the meeting what you expect. Please, simply listen or offer thoughts. Springing your purpose in the middle of your hoopla regarding which role you want your guest to take is unfair and can be actually embarrassing. For example, what if your guest has been daydreaming or just half-listening to your concerns? Oops! Caught goofing off. Imagine the embarrassment when you ask for advice. But the blame cannot be placed entirely on your sandbox friend: you and I have to establish our intentions at the beginning of the conversation. Remember that our concerns and problems just may not be all that exciting and intriguing to our friend, so don't become offended if the friend is caught off-guard. However, one thing is certain: God cares! And listens!

"Morning, noon, and night I complain and groan, and He listens to my voice." - Psalm 55:17

Hurt feelings are bound to happen from time-to-time. But we must protect and preserve our sandbox. We must be the ones in charge. When we take control of our sandbox, we are able to diminish our stress level. So many stressful issues can occur in our lives when we are not in control of our sandbox. By opening up the floodgates of our personal sandbox to one and all, we are headed for disaster.

Be aware of the verbal grenade that can be thrown into your sandbox. The explosion may well come from uninvited family members. Some members may believe that our sandbox also belongs to them, then our boundaries may not always be honored. Boom! They may try to convince us that they have profound interest, kindhearted intentions, and personal concerns for our well-being which, of course, is very commendable. However, it doesn't mean that they have the privilege of entering our sandbox at any time. They may not be observing our invisible sign that says: NOT WELCOME. We must be very careful and loving when we are involved in such a familial situation.

Do not try being a therapist within your family circle. There can be too many mental and emotional setbacks. First of all, we place ourselves above the one we are striving to help. Certainly an excellent way of not being invited to the family Christmas dinner.

Secondly, to whomever we are imparting our gems of wisdom and experiences can turn the tables. They may actually know too much about us—our past miserable experiences, our unending faults, our untruths. All of a sudden it is our head that ends up on the chopping block, and our beloved family member has a hand on the guillotine.

Thirdly, we can create a miserable strain on the relationship since we will have private, intimate information about that particular family member.

Lastly, what happens when the family member decides not to follow our gems of wisdom? Are we really going to be able to accept whatever decisions the person makes? How do you say, "Resentment" in a nice way? In our family circle, we cannot have complete objectivity, so churning out advice will be somewhat one-sided. With knowledge comes power. And there might be the tendency on our part to use such power to manipulate the very one we are helping.

In plain words: Don't attempt to become a therapist to your kinfolks. There are plenty of good therapists for them in whom to select. It is fine to be an attentive listener but be very, very cautious when you find yourself in the advice-giving category. The last thing you want to do is to make them feel guilty when they don't change.

You have the right to make the choice that will change your life.

Suggestions: *Establish your boundaries clearly and early.*
                 Explain the Sandbox to family and friends.
                 Enter another person's sandbox carefully.
                 Be more of a listener than an advice-giver.
                 Know your own limitations when your friend is seeking advice and guidance.

No one wants to be around grumpy people—young or old. As seen in the next chapter, you don't need a therapist to help yourself with your irritable self.

CHAPTER 2
NO- NONSENSE IRRITABILITY

Life is a banquet, and most people
are starving to death.

--Auntie Mame
(one of my favorite movies)

Dedicated to my Youth Board Presidents
at North East Park Baptist Church who
tried to keep me from Irritability.

Jim Nash, Craig Soderquist, Billy
Ellis, David Frakes, Sid Webb,
David McAuley, Chet Thompson

CHAPTER 2

We have heard repeatedly throughout our lives that life is what you make of it. For the most part it can be wholesome, fun, and adventuresome. On the other hand, it can also be dreary, stressful, and downright depressing. Unless there is something drastically wrong with a person, no one wishes for a life of misery, frustration, and anger. However, it is true that even the happiest, stress-free person can at times become irritated. Over what? Anything, absolutely anything. We seek to live the life that Auntie Mame described as being a banquet...lots of things to do, to see, to be a part of. However, there are times when we get just plain grumpy and downright irritable.

A junk collector was pushing his cart along the sidewalk and collecting items he could sell or cash in for deposits. He came to a woman sweeping the walk and called out, *"Any old beer bottles, madam?"* The woman frowned. *"How dare you! Do I look like the type of woman who would drink beer?"* The collector made a mock bow, *"Pardon me, Madam. I was mistaken. Any old vinegar bottles and pickle jars?"* (Sourcebook of Humor)

There are basically four ways in which to deal with one's irritability. Our irritable moods can be traced to one or more causes. Identifying the four is not, however, enough. We also need to know how to do something about our irritability before our friends run for the hills. **HALT** is the magic word.

Whenever we know that we are entering the canyon of irritability, we need to determine which letter(s) in **HALT** is creating our problem. Once that has been determined, we can do something positive to return ourselves into our comfy arena. It isn't that difficult to place our finger on the cause. Our irritability is identical to that of having a baby or child in our home.

H – Hunger

H in the word *halt* stands for **Hunger.** Identical to that of a baby. When our hunger signals go off, we need food. Whether it is a snack or a meal, the basic need for food must be satisfied...or else... our irritability will manifest itself intensely and be known to those around us. Irritability can rear its ugly face quickly when our need for some type of nourishment is required.

A mother was pleading with her young son to eat his spinach. *"Come on, Johnny,"* she begged. *"Think of the thousands of children in the under-developed countries who would love some nice spinach like this."* Johnny looked up and demanded, *"Name two."* (The Sourcebook of Humor)

Several months ago, the **H** hit me full force. I was getting into my car from the grocery store, late at night, and out of nowhere, I became very irritable. I was still several miles from home. Immediately I went through **HALT** and knew what was going on: I was starving. So out of my grocery bag came a much needed candy bar. While the result is far from a Biblical miracle, I was amazed at how fast my irritability disappeared once I had devoured the chocolate bar. In my case, chocolate was the miracle! My raunchy mood became past tense. When you and I are hungry, our sour mood will dissipate once we have something to digest.

A hungry gentleman sitting under the stars with his dog lit a candle and opened a date to eat. It was full of worms, so he tossed it to his dog. The same was true of the second and the third. So, he blew out the candle, stopped looking at the stars, then opened the fourth date and ate it while his dog gave him a snaring look. (Sourcebook of Humor). Obviously the master was becoming hungry and irritable and needed that last date, much to the chagrin of his dog.

Suggestion for H: If your irritability is due to hunger, grab something to eat as quickly as you can. Your world will immediately become brighter for you and for those around you.

A – Anger

The second letter in **HALT** can become a more challenging category to handle than hunger. First of all, we have to own our feeling of anger without feeling guilty about it. It is not an emotion to be ashamed of, but it is a powerful emotion which means that we need to be very careful on how we express it.

Secondly, we need to decide where our anger is coming from. Did someone cross your path at work the wrong way? Did some event take place that rattled you on your trip to the grocery store? Before you left your home in the morning, did anything or anyone cause you to become angry?

****

Be not angry that you cannot make others as you wish them to be, since you cannot make yourself as you wish to be.

--Thomas A Kempis

****

Thirdly, once we own the anger and realize where it originated, we will have to decide what to do with it. Perhaps we need to face the person who created the problem? Maybe a situation in our life needs to be changed? Until we are able to determine the cause of the anger, our irritability is fast at work. It continues to become more and more volatile while we are waiting to put a halt to our nasty mood. Quickly putting a closure on the anger and stopping the irritability require facing the anger head-on and deciding what to do with it.

****

Anger tortures itself.

--Publilius Syrus

****

One family in the neighborhood kept their household from overheating from fits of anger by using this solution: Whenever one of the three boys was mad enough to boil over, he went to the refrigerator, got an egg, and started walking toward a big oak tree on the far side of their lot. As he walked, he tried to squeeze the egg in the palm of his hand, trying as hard as he could to break it. Usually by the time he reached the oak tree, he felt foolish enough to be calmed down. But if he was still angry, he was allowed to throw the egg against the oak tree. If the anger was gone, he brought the egg back to the refrigerator. *"We raised three wonderful boys,"* the mother says, *"and lost very few eggs."* (A Dictionary of Illustrations)

Suggestions for A: Talk to someone you trust to vent your anger.
Write on paper what is causing the anger.
Do some type of physical exertion to reduce the anger.
Confront the person if absolutely necessary.
Own your anger.

L – Loneliness

Everyone on planet earth has to deal with loneliness from time-to-time. It is no respecter of persons. It can occur in babies, children, adolescents, and adults—in marriage and in single life. It can create a sad, dreary feeling. It sometimes becomes an emotion that we simply have to "ride through" until we get to the other side.

****

It is proper and beneficial
sometimes to be left to thyself.

--Thomas A Kempis

****

Loneliness can disturb our peaceful souls and stir up dismal feelings. Even in a room filled with people we love, we can still feel lonely. It doesn't provide us much notice that it's waiting at our doorstep. It knocks and comes right on in. As a result we may feel like a survivor on a deserted island. This category of irritability has a double whammy. On one hand we feel lonely while at the same time our irritable mood is constructing a wall between others and us.

The real challenge in dealing with loneliness is realizing that we need to have some type of contact with a living creature and then actually doing it. Our loneliness is propelling us toward receiving some type of attention. Whether it's a pet or a person, we crave the acknowledgment. In my own life, there have been times when I would go to the airport just to sit and to watch—I just needed to have my loneliness taken care of. My irritability had separated me temporarily from friends because of my irritating mood. I knew that to solve the problem of loneliness and to get rid of the irritability, it would require my being in the midst of others.

Loneliness can be paralyzing because one feels miserable and forgotten. One thing is for certain: you cannot halt your irritability until the loneliness is taken care of. You and I may feel lonely and forsaken, but you and I are never alone. God is always with us no matter how lonely we feel:

"I will never leave thee, nor forsake thee." – Hebrews 13:5

Loneliness occurs in the young, old, poor, rich, and famous. In the book, <u>Invitation—Billy Graham and the Lives God Touched</u>, the authors Basyle and Adam Tchividjian (grandsons of Billy Graham) tell the story of Dr. Graham being in south Florida for a board meeting.

While there, Dr. Graham was feeling lonely. He knew what to do—he looked up some friends who lived nearby and went for a visit.

(The following words are to be found engraved on the floor of
the church where John Wesley preached his first sermon.)

Enter this door
As if the floor
Within were gold
And every wall
of jewels, all-knowing
Of wealth untold;
As if a choir
In robes of fire
Were singing here
Nor shout, nor rush
But hush--
For God is here. (--author unknown)

*Suggestions for L: Visit a friend.
Call someone.
Go somewhere there are people.
Play with your pets.
Invite guests into your home.*

T – Tired

When we were babies, our parents knew how irritable we could become unless we got a nap. The same is true of all ages. Our bodies demand an adequate amount of sleep. This is certainly not a "no-brainer" but sometimes we forget to oil and to tune up our bodies—with rest. When we push ourselves to the "nth" degree, without adequate sleep or rest, the body may have a meltdown. It is tired, exhausted. And it demands our attention—sleep. When the body is forced to keep operating past adequate sleep, it does its natural thing: meanness, irritability.

We can actually become mean-spirited towards others and ourselves. In some cultures, time during the work hours is given for naps. What a brilliant idea! Unfortunately in our American society, taking a nap while working is a no-no. Thus, this category of irritability can be difficult to solve since we are expected to be alert at work, not napping. The problem: managing the irritability until sleep is acquired. And since we cannot get 40 winks at work, we may need to splash cold water on our faces or whatever else does the trick. We have to bide our time until z-z-z-z-z-z-z.

Suggestions for T: *Get the sleep your body needs.*
Rest during your work breaks. Take a stroll.
When possible, walk even when tired.
Stay positive and don't give in to your exhaustion.

You may find, at times, that you can't place the cause of your irritability into any of the four categories. That will be a rare occasion. Two of the categories (hunger and tiredness) are physical in scope while the other two (anger and loneliness) are both mental and emotional. By far, the anger and loneliness will present the greatest challenge in which to confront. The reason is that each one has layers. With anger, you may be disappointed in someone or disgusted with yourself for being in a negative situation. Or perhaps you may feel mistreated, discouraged, or betrayed. Any number of negative emotions could set the stage for the explosion of anger. If the anger has been allowed to fester, then the irritability can emerge full blown.

The same can be said of loneliness. Perhaps you have felt neglected, ostracized, or insulted. These feelings can certainly establish the emotion of loneliness.

When hunger and tiredness are the prevailing reasons for our irritable nature, they usually do not carry extra burdens of hidden feelings. Their solutions can be rather simple: food and rest/sleep.

The wonderful news about the **HALT** syndrome is God's provision for us. In eternity past, God looked down the corridors of time and knew absolutely what we humans would experience—bouts of irritability. Rather than leaving it entirely up to us to find the means of coping, God's grace provided the answers.

Hunger – Intake Food

"He gives food to every living creature—
because his mercy endures forever."

Psalm 136:25

H

A

L

T

Anger – Own it, deal with it

"Let go of anger, and leave rage behind. Do not
be preoccupied. It only causes harm."

Psalm 37:8

HALT

Loneliness – Seek out companionship

*"Even if my father and mother abandon me,
the Lord will take care of me."*

Psalm 27:10

H

A

L

T

Tiredness – Rest/sleep

*"God gives strength to those who grow tired and
increases the strength of those who are weak."*

Isaiah 40:29

**Be realistic. You really don't have
all the time in the world.**

CHAPTER 3

NO-NONSENSE TIME AWARENESS

Time is really the only capital that any human being has and the thing that one can least afford to waste or lose.

---Thomas Edison

Dedicated to my phenomenal parents who gave me their time and love.

CHAPTER 3

When we were young, we viewed time totally different than later in life. As young people, our concept of time was based on how quickly we got what we wanted or how slowly we were made to wait. As we got older, time became more valuable. We began to understand that time was either friendly or hostile, depending on how we were using it. As a friendly commodity, we accomplished a truck-load of tasks. From dawn's early light we were off and running, maintaining personal and family relationships, doing necessary errands, and enjoying pleasure activities. Time was indeed our friend.

****

Time is so precious that God deals it out only second by second.

--Bishop Fulton J. Sheen

****

At the end of the day, we would smile. Time had been good to us. We had the opportunity to produce positive results of our use of time. Our day turned out to be good, based on our positive experiences and accomplishments. We would pat ourselves on the back because we had successfully utilized our waking hours. All seemed well in our universe. Hallelujah!

Now, if only every solitary day could turn out so well. When we rise each morning we fully intend to use our time wisely. Very few of us greet the morning with an attitude of *"I hope today is miserable and chaotic. I aim to make a mockery of my life, and when possible, I want to cause havoc in the lives of others." "I want as much stress as I can get today."*

Time is an awesome commodity. It permits us to be active or passive, people-centered or task-centered, self-centered or not, alone or not. While there are moments in the day when our schedules (and bosses) dictate our activities, we are still the ultimate masters of our time in the sense that we are in control of our daily lives.

A mother was teaching her daughter how to tell time. *"There are the minutes and there are the seconds,"* she said. *"But Mama,"* the daughter asked, *"Where are the jiffies?"* (Sourcebook of Humor) Our presence may be restricted to one space but not our thought-processing. At any waking moment in time, we have jurisdiction of our thoughts. While we may be in the most boring meeting of the ages (and I have), we can be anywhere else on the globe, doing anything we want, and be with whomever—in our creative minds. Time cannot limit our minds. We are free agents. For the most part, how we spend our time physically is ultimately up to us.

Son: *"Daddy, may I ask you a question?"*

Dad: *"Yeah sure, what is it?"*

Son: *"Daddy, how much do you make an hour?"*

Dad: *"That's none of your business. Why do you ask such a thing?"*

Son: *"I just want to know. Please tell me how much do you make an hour?"*

Dad: *"If you must know, I make $100 an hour."*

Son: *"Oh!"* (with his head down)

Dr. Ray Ashurst, Ph.D.

Son: *"Daddy, may I please borrow $50?"* The father was furious.

Dad: *"If the only reason you asked that is so you can borrow some money to buy a silly toy or some other nonsense, then you march yourself straight to your room and go to bed. Think about why you are being so selfish. I work hard everyday for such childish behavior."*

The little boy quietly went to his room and shut the door.

The father sat down and started to get even angrier about the little boy's questions. How dare he ask such questions only to get some money.

After about an hour or so, the man had calmed down, and started to think: *"Maybe there was something the boy really needed to buy with that $50, and he really didn't ask for money very often."* The father went to the door of the little boy's room and opened the door.

Dad: *"Are you asleep, son?"*

Son: *"No daddy. I'm awake."*

Dad: *"I've been thinking, son. Maybe I was too hard on you earlier. It's been a long day, and I took out my aggravation on you. Here's the $50 you asked for."*

The little boy sat straight up, smiling.

Son: *"Oh, thank you, Daddy!"*

Then reaching under his pillow the boy pulled out some crumpled up bills. The father saw that the boy already had money. He started to get angry again. The little boy counted out his money, and then looked up at his father.

Dad: *"Why do you want more money if you already have some?"*

Son: *"Because I didn't have enough, but now I do. Daddy, I have $100 now. Can I buy an hour of your time? Please come home early tomorrow. I would like to have dinner with you."*

The father was crushed. He put his arms around his little son, and he begged for his forgiveness. (Lycia Marie)

26

"If you had a bank that credited your account each morning with $86,400, that carried no balance from day to day, allowed you to keep no cash in your account, and finally every evening canceled whatever part of the amount you had failed to use during the day, what would you do? Draw out every cent—of course! Well, you have such a bank and its name is "Time." Every morning it credits you with 86,400 seconds. Every night it rules off—as lost—whatever of this you have failed to invest to good purpose. It carries no balance. It allows no balances. It allows no overdrafts. Each day the bank named "Time" opens a new account with you. Each night it burns the records of the day. If you fail to use the day's deposits, the loss is yours. There is no going back. There is no drawing against tomorrow. You must live in the present—on today's deposits. Invest it so as to get from it the utmost in health, happiness, and success." (Robert G. Lee)

We are consciously made aware of time especially by our family and friends.

A small boy comes downstairs one Sunday morning, leaving the rest of the family asleep. The clock was striking eight but was out of order. As it struck nine, ten, eleven, twelve, thirteen, fourteen, the boy's wonder grew. Finally he turned and faced upstairs calling: *"Get up, quick! It's later than it's ever been.!"* (Dictionary of Illustrations)

Time is the most priceless gem we own. However, it cannot be saved for a better day or frozen, banked, or temporarily put on hold. We cannot rent, buy, or store it. Time carries no balances into our new day. There is no going back to yesterday to retrieve our time, and there is no securing time against tomorrow's account. It is irrevocable, irreclaimable, and irreplaceable. Time is our "here and now" property. Time can be our Friend because we are able to accomplish our daily goals and to become a better person within ourselves and in our relationships. It is what we do with our time that matters so much in our daily lives. And yet it can easily slip away or be wasted.

Wasting time is the most extravagant
and costly of all expenses.

--Anonymous

"You wake up in the morning, and lo! Your purse (wallet) is magically filled with twenty-four hours of the magic tissue of the universe of your life. No one can take it from you. It is uneatable. No one receives either more or less than you receive. Waste your infinitely precious commodity as much as you will, and the supply will never be withheld from you. Moreover, you cannot draw on the future.

It is impossible to get into debt. You can only waste the passing moment. You cannot waste tomorrow; it is kept for you." (Arnold Bennett)

In our younger days, we thought we had all the time in the world to carry out our wishes. As the years accumulated, we realized that Time does not work that way. We are held accountable. Some of us fidget away precious time, and what is very sad is that we know we are doing it. At our early age, we are constantly told to beware of time. Whether it was to be home on time or to get our homework finished, we knew that time was of the essence. And all of us had to make a decision—use our time wisely or not.

A motorist far from home was taking a detour along a country road that ran between two highways. Spotting a farmer swinging on his front porch, the motorist stopped to ask what time it was. *"Twelve o'clock,"* said the farmer without breaking his swing. *"Only twelve o'clock,"* the motorist said. *"I was sure it was more than that."* *"Nope, it's never more than that around here. It goes up to twelve o'clock and then starts all over again."* (James Hefley)

God instructs us to use time wisely because we have no idea when it can be in jeopardy.

"Redeeming the time because the days are evil." – Ephesians 5:16

There are time when we need to reflect and to be still. Going 24/7 will wear us down after a certain amount of time. It is impossible to hear what God is trying to tell us when we are always on the move. God has to ring our chimes to get our attention. And sometimes those chimes mean going through some intense heartbreaks and emotional hurt. God wants us to hear Him, and that means we have to slow down or get to our special "quiet spot" to receive the message.

****

Sometimes I just sit and stare, and not think. Afterwards, I feel better.

--Jenna West

****

Time is a non-nonsense element: it is reality, it is neutral, it is no respecter of persons, and it just happens. We may not be able to make sense of what happens with our time, but it nevertheless happens. How many hours do we spend trying to figure out why things happened at particular times? Hours and hours, wondering why. Time does not have a conscience, so it does not owe us an explanation. It just happens. Our challenge is to use it in a just and wise manner and to allow God to be in control of our daily lives.

"Today is here. I will start with a smile and resolve to be agreeable. I will not criticize. I refuse to waste my valuable time.

Today is one thing I know I am equal with all others—time. All of us draw the same salary in seconds, minutes, and hours.

Today I will not waste my time because the minutes I wasted yesterday are as lost as a vanished thought.

Today I refuse to spend time worrying about what might happen—it usually doesn't. I am going to spend time making things happen.

Today I am determined to study to improve myself, for tomorrow I may be wanted, and I must not be found lacking.

Today I am determined to do the things that I should do. I firmly determine to stop doing the things I should not do.

Today I begin by doing and not wasting my time. In one week I will be miles beyond the person I am today.

Today I will not imagine what I would do if things were different. They are not different. I will make success with what material I have.

*Today I will stop saying "If I had time--" I know
I never will "find time" for anything. If I want time, I
must make it.*

*Today I will act towards other people as though
this might be my last day on earth. I will not wait for
tomorrow. Tomorrow never comes."* (Gerald B. Klein)

No one can predict how much time we have on earth, but the exciting thing is that we are alive right now. Each day is a blessing and can only be seen as such when we respect time and use it effectively. We simply do not have "the time" to waste and to be ingrates. Each day is given to us as a gift from God.

The names of the clients in this book have been changed to protect the innocent...as well as the guilty.

Seth referred himself to me with the naïve intention of coming to therapy for only a few sessions. He thought that his personal concerns could certainly be ironed out quickly and firmly. He viewed therapy as if he were ordering a meal at a local Burger King. Drive in, place your order, pay at the first window, pick up the order at the second window, and then gun it past the kids' play yard in front of the restaurant into traffic. He lived with the slogan: "Have it my way."

I really could not fault Seth regarding his belief that therapy was a quickie and that he was the boss when sitting in a therapy setting. Probably many folks who wander into therapy feel the same way. Seth was twenty-two, gun-ho, assertive, and almost aggressive, and tight with his finances. He had been reared in an era in which he believed that he was entitled to whatever he desired without "blood, sweat, and tears." Furthermore, Seth expected whatever he wanted to be immediately fulfilled, with full respect to his busy life schedule. He expected things to be done quickly and to his exact specifications: plus very inexpensive and definitely with no hassle.

Little did Seth realize that his expectations of therapy were going to hit the big life fan once he chose to travel the therapy road. He needed to buckle up because it was definitely going to be a bumpy ride. Seth was brought up in a household that viewed life's deadlines as the time to actually begin the expected responsibilities and not when they were actually due. Being the only offspring, Seth's viewpoint of time was created, maintained, and encouraged wholeheartedly by his laid-back parents. Their parenting skills were quite decent, but Seth had not been introduced adequately to the importance of time management and its twin sister, time awareness.

During Seth's formative years, he was not held accountable to the usefulness of his personal time. His life had a lazy tone to it, and unfortunately at that time, it served Seth quite well. He would portray this attitude to his friends, family, and himself. His idea of time had a colorful flair to it since there was very little accountability expected from his parents.

As Seth reached an ever-demanding stage of adolescence, he began to feel misplaced and misguided, within a maze of confusion and helplessness. His parents did not detect Seth's quandary of panic and hopelessness. His concept and usefulness of time began gradually to place him on a roller coaster ride, spiraling downward. His teachers, friends, bosses, and coaches expected Seth to honor the code of doing projects on time and of being specific places on time. Seth could no longer use his normal faithful excuses to account for his laid-back lifestyle. His handy-dandy, pull out an excuse syndrome would no longer work and be acceptable. It became time to face the music realistically, and to Seth, such an expectation contained discordant sounds, something similar to a student of the violin at one's first unforgettable lesson.

By the time Seth entered into his twenties, he realized that life, as he knew it thus far, was not like a riding lawnmower but rather an old, worn out weed eater. The weeds represented his poor choices of time management skills and the stress he was living under. He was trying to cope with an inability of making his time a well-guarded friend, rather than a constant enemy. His futile attempts to explain away his poor intentions of punctuality and reliability to others fell on barren ground. His world of friends and acquaintances was turning quickly into an Armageddon—desertion, confusion, chaos, frightening, and destruction.

At this moment in Seth's historical arena, he became one of my most challenging clients. Why? It was due to Seth living in his world of "time chaos" which meant he had to attempt re-arranging his priorities and re-organizing his brain format. This definitely was not a walk in the park. His attitude towards time was that of a young lad and not that of a young adult man. It was no surprise that he existed in a world of panic, extreme anxiety, and frustration. He obviously was not competent in any degree of time management or time awareness. He blamed others for his lack of time awareness and was angry about his friends deserting him. Seth was a daily victim of his lack of understanding the value of time. He just had never acquired the skills of making his time behave and obedient to the expectations of the society in which he lived.

The sessions with Seth were a mixture of having "light bulb" moments, gnashing of teeth of guilt and anger, and pushing forth the need for newer and better choices. His therapeutic journey was not an overnight success nor a brief moment in history. It took time. A lot of time. Making new choices and actually activating them can be tedious and frustrating, with long hours of diligent effort, especially when the journey involves mind-altering. For Seth to have a more abundant life, it required a dedicated and committed effort on his part—which he did.

Seth had the necessary will-power to stick it out to the finishing line. However, his journey had many roadblocks. His mental roadblocks attempted to turn Seth towards distractions, such as quitting his journey all together or catapulting him into his familiar role of a victim.

The old adage can be said to be true for Seth: if he can do it, anyone can. Seth had been firmly planted and situated in his own encompassing world of time awareness. It is true that not everyone's makeup is geared towards a structured, scheduled lifestyle. Some of us seem to do much better by being spontaneous and highly flexible. Such was Seth's way of doing things. Therefore, the goal in Seth's therapy was not to attack and to devour his preferred style of living. Rather, it was to introduce ways in which time was not his enemy but a competent life stronghold. Time takes on the personality we give it, and there is absolutely no reason that it can't be utilized effectively, in a wholesome way. Time, in and of itself, was never meant to be a cause of anxiety and madness. We humans are the barometers of our personal time management--it can be our friend or our enemy.

You and I have the ability and privilege to **Stop** allowing time making us a victim. We have the internal power to be in charge of the way in which we manage our personal time.

You are only a breath away from changing your life.

Stand

Tall

On

Principles

****

Tomorrow is the most important thing in life. Comes unto us at midnight very clean. It's perfect when it arrives and it puts itself in our hands. It hopes we've learned something from yesterday.

--John Wayne

****

Suggestions: *Keep a daily schedule of your use of time, and at the close of each day, analyze it.*
Purchase books on the "how to" use time successfully.
Realize that you and your time are accountable to God.
Go over your schedule with a close friend and ask for suggestions.
If you are wasting too much time, find projects to do which have deadlines.

Want to know where your real power is?
The next chapter answers the question.

CHAPTER 4

NO-NONSENSE POWER

Grow old gracefully, showering grace on those we love. We must bathe them in grace like those who believe that grace is limitless. Show everyone I meet with more affection than they would expect, more than they have any right to, more than I have ever given anyone ever in my life.

--Andrew Greeley

Dedicated to my Youth Board Presidents at Dale City Baptist Church who empowered me to guide them.

Mike Burrow, Richard Pannell, Jeff Hosfeld, Mark Yates, Darrell Burrow, Tim Spence, Bruce Evatt

CHAPTER 4

When our Creator formed us, He did not want us to be His puppets on a string. He breathe into us a free will in which to make our individual decisions and to accomplish whatever goals we had. Our free will allowed us to be authentic, autonomous beings. He bestowed upon us a free reign in which we have the ultimate authority to govern our lives as we see fit. No two people are the same. With this free will comes an inner power that permits us to think, to feel, and to act as individual agents. Free will and inner power go hand-in-hand. They belong together. From the time of our birth we have free will and inner power to decide for ourselves what we wish to do, what we need to think about, and whatever emotions we choose to have at any point in time.

However, life provides a multitude of distractions. And these distractions can cause us to run amuck, and at times we find ourselves giving our inner power away to others. And these individuals end up running and controlling our lives: when we are to think, what we are to feel, and how we are to act according to their wishes. We still have free will, but the moment we give away our power, then our free will suffers from confusion and distractions. As we mature into adulthood we can use our inner power to enhance our lives.

The meaning of inner power is simple: we are entitled to think what we want to think, to feel what we want to feel, and to do what we need to do.

Power = our thoughts, feelings, actions

If we are to grow and to develop in a healthy way, we must maintain our inner power by not giving it to others.

However, for one reason or the othe, we have the tendency to discard our inner power by giving it to others and becoming self-proclaimed victims: it's also called the self-pity syndrome. *"Woe is me." "I've always been a mess." "Everybody picks on me."* Feeling self-pitiful can become eventually our comfort zone in life. It gives us the attention we crave, good or bad. We can thrive on our self-pity. Because we have given away our power for years, we have forgotten what using one's inner power is like. We have become quite cozy in the victim role, so thus we remain. Sadly, all of us have individuals in our lives who would like to snatch away our power. In that way, they can become controllers of our thoughts, emotions, and actions.

Stop blaming others for what you have or don't have, or for what you feel or don't feel. When you blame others for what you're going through, you deny responsibility and perpetuate the problem. Stop giving your power away and start taking responsibility for your life. Blaming is just another sorry excuse, and

making excuses is the first step towards failures. You and only you are responsible for your life choices and decisions.

---Marc Chernoff

It is indeed a sorrowful picture when we continue to give away our power to others. We live and breathe under their shadows. What we do, where we go, the way we think, and even how we feel are all up for grabs. The individuals dictate our thoughts, feelings, and actions because they have taken over our power. We have given it to them, and they love it. They become our controllers which means they become all-powerful over us. We live under stress and become their victims.

Not using this Life Skill of maintaining one's power is very dangerous because unless we use it, we do not have a ghost of a chance of utilizing the other Life Skills effectively. You and I must be in control of our thoughts, feelings, and actions and accountable. God never ever intended for us to be another person's puppet. He designed us to be strong, to serve others, to be autonomous individuals, and to be confident in ourselves.

Be sober (stable), be vigilant (alert), because your adversary, the devil, like a roaring lion walketh about, seeking whom he may devour. – I Peter 5:8

We have the right, responsibility, and privilege of proclaiming ourselves as sovereign individuals. With such comes the freedom of our personal and individual thoughts, emotions, and actions.

****

He is truly great in power who has power over himself.

--Charles Haddon Spurgeon

****

You and I have the right to exercise our power. By owning our own thoughts without being harassed, of experiencing our emotions without being condemned, and of carrying out our ethical actions without being persecuted is what our inner power is all about.

On the flip side of the coin is the person who tosses away the inner power to just anyone. Why would an individual wish to remain a victim? Why would the person prefer feeling self-pity? What does the person achieve from being a victim rather than exercising one's inner power?

Being victims not only brings forth negative attention, but it also permits us to blame everyone else for our shortcomings, problems, and failures. Victims are blamers. They believe that everything happening badly in their life is someone else's fault. *"Others are at fault for my topsy-turvy world,"* is the attitude that they have...and actually believe.

The victim becomes so accustomed to being in a subservient role that the cause of one's negative emotions are attributed to others. It's like pulling a life blanket over one's head and hiding away from responsibilities, routines, and relationships. If I become a victim, I can escape from accountability and live a life of denial and pity. The victim soon becomes a shadow of a person, of what one was, surrounded by controlling family members, friends, and authoritative persons. It doesn't take long before the victim turns into a co-dependent, self-contained figure in society. Tragically, the victim succumbs to those he has bestowed the power to. And the controllers in turn instruct the victim how he should think, feel, and behave.

> **Don't try to avoid experiencing whatever you're experiencing. If you're angry, frustrated, disgusted, resentful, despairing, whatever it is, let yourself feel it—but also know that you can detach from it. If you don't let yourself really experience what's going on, it won't be clear what you're detaching from.**
>
> *--Morrie Schwartz*

We can actually hear people giving up their power in their conversations:

> *"He made me so mad."*
> *"She made me furious!"*
> *"They ganged up on me and made me discouraged."*
> *"I used to think it was crazy, but she told me I was wrong,*
> *so, I guess I believe her."*
> *"I had no intentions of going there, but he said*
> *I was being foolish, so I went."*
> *"I haven't been to church lately, and they made me feel guilty."*

****

If you can't stand yourself,
neither can anybody else.

--Sid Caesar

****

No one but no one has the power to make you feel any emotion. We choose that emotion. It is always our choice. We find convenient scapegoats for our negative feelings, always blaming someone else. The simple truth is that we selected that particular emotion. Our supervisor says something to us that we don't particularly like, so in turn we stick that person with a particular feeling. *"He made me furious."* In reality, no, he didn't. We chose being furious rather than choosing not to be. Our supervisor doesn't have that supreme power (even though he may think he does.). No one but no human being has that kind of power! We have the freedom to choose our personal feelings, thoughts, and actions. This is a Life Skill that we may not particularly like because we have to be accountable for our emotions, our actions, and our thoughts which in turn means to stop blaming others.

Directing your emotions involves working through on an emotional level the issues that you confront and having enough emotional space, so to speak, to handle these issues without being overwhelmed by them. By 'emotional space' I mean that you're not locked into a particular way of feeling and thinking, that you

43

> ***can see and connect with alternatives.***
> ***You can exercise considerable influence***
> ***over your emotions by recognizing***
> ***that you have emotional choices.***
>
> ***--Morrie Schwartz***

It is not easy at times to maintain one's inner power. There may be moments when we would rather throw up our hands, quit, and deny our power. Let someone else be in charge of my life for a little while. Feeling this way is quite normal and even expected at times in our lives. But beware of the danger of thinking such. We were created as independent individuals who were given a healthy functioning mind in which to own our individual thoughts, feelings, and behavior.

> ***God desires us to face our feelings with power and trust.***
> ***He wants us to own our thoughts with authority and confidence.***
> ***We are to act on a spiritual level that continuously honors Him.***

Paul Dietzel, head football coach at the University of South Carolina, former All-American and "Coach of the Year," says: *"When I surrendered my life to Christ, I pledged myself to measure my actions and plans by the Life and Person of Christ. But I've found that I can't discipline myself by myself. I only strangle when I start to pull myself up by my own neck. I must have help from above. Too many people think of Jesus as an effeminate weakling. But I don't believe this for a minute. Look at Jesus. As a carpenter, He did hard manual labor—without modern power tools. Everywhere He went He walked. Once He fasted for forty days and nights to prepare Himself for His work. He overthrew the money-changers in the temple. He was tortured by the soldiers and made to carry a heavy cross. He hung for six hours in awful agony without a word of complaint. How weak He makes all of us by comparison. Neither do I think of the Christian as a weak person. Meekness does not mean weakness.*

The Bible teaches that the Christian should live a harnessed, self-disciplined, self-contained life. I have pledge to submit my body as a living sacrifice to Jesus Christ. As an athlete and leader I try to be what I ask my players to be." (Play Ball)

And you and I are commanded by God to emulate the type of life that Coach Dietzel is talking about. It is a dynamic challenge for all of us, not to even mention what an exciting journey it can be.

There may be times when we are placed into situations that are not our choosing. However, by maintaining our inner power, we are free to choose how we will respond. **No matter what**: the important lesson is not to give away our power just because we are involved in circumstances due to someone else. You and you alone have the power to react or to respond in the manner you choose.

If you and I are determined to sustain ourselves with our inner power, which will cut through our daily stress, then we are obligated to acknowledge and to own our individual feelings, actions, and thoughts.

Suggestions: *Be alert to what situations and individuals deprived you of your power.*
Once you know you have given your power away, back up and retrieve it.
Ask close friends to let you know when you have given away your power.
Get professional guidance if you need it.
Read positive books on inner power.

Keep a daily journal of the times you have kept your power and the times you haven't.
Pray that God will make you more like Him.

Want to feel good about yourself?
Want to believe you are worthwhile?
What do your tapes say?
The next chapter will help you
with such questions.

CHAPTER 5

NO-NONSENSE TAPES

We cannot learn without pain.

--Aristotle

Dedicated to all my clients who
have become my friends.

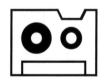

CHAPTER 5

Ninety-five percent of the beliefs we have stored in our minds are nothing but lies, and we suffer because we believe all these lies.

---Don Miguel Ruiz

Our chance for ultimate happiness in life was designed long ago. We are promised the pursuit of happiness:

"We hold these truths to be self-evident, that all men are created equal, that they are endowed by their creator with certain unalienable Rights, that among these are Life, Liberty, and the pursuit of Happiness."

In eternity past, God bequeathed happiness to all believers in Him:

"A merry heart doeth good like a medicine." – Proverbs 17:22

If you and I are guaranteed the Divine unalienable right for a "merry heart" by our Sovereign God, then what keeps us from that precious happiness? That happiness we spend much of our lives trying to snag and to keep? Genuine happiness has absolutely nothing to do with external sources, such as money, automobiles, jobs, homes—absolutely none of these things carry a Certificate of

Happiness attached. We are made to believe by societal standards that such things will give us everlasting happiness. So, gullible and desperate as we are at times, with credit card in hand, we head out shopping for that one thing we believe will make us happy.

Once there was a little puppy chasing its tail. It kept chasing its tail all day long, day after day.

The puppy never seemed to tire of chasing it. But one day a large dog stopped near where the puppy was, and the puppy stopped long enough to have a short conversation with the large dog. The large dog said to the puppy, *"Why are you always chasing your tail?"* *"Well,"* answered the puppy, *"when I was a very young puppy I learned that happiness was in my tail. So as long as it was up and wagging, I was happy. When it dropped, or fell between my legs, I was not so happy. So I've just decided to always chase my tail, since that is my source of happiness. But the trouble is that I never really catch it!"* The older and more mature dog said to the puppy, *"When I was a puppy like you, that's exactly the way I thought too. But one day I forgot to chase my tail. And, lo and behold, when I looked around, happiness was following me wherever I went."* (C. Edward Houk)

Isn't it true to life that after the newness of our purchase wears off, we are on our search again? Why? Because we believe that happiness is external, and that we can capture it. But the truth is that our happiness is internal. Always has been and always will be. Happiness is such an overworked word: we are happy to get a nap, happy to locate an address, happy to feel the sun's warmth, happy to be remembered on our birthday, happy to be eating a certain food. Perhaps a better word would be "contentment" since it means being at ease or satisfied with oneself

"What is keeping us from being happy or contented?"

****

Life is a journey, not a destination.
Happiness is not "there," but here,
not tomorrow, but today.

--Sidney Greenberg

****

One of the reasons for our continual stress and our frantic search for happiness can be summed up as our "life tapes" which began at birth and continues until we draw our last breath. "Tapes" are the messages that we have been told, shown, or felt by those in our life arena—positive and negative—from our parents, siblings, relatives, teachers, friends, preachers—everyone. Every single message has been stored in our minds—every last one. While some made us very happy, others did not.

To fully understand the magnitude and power of our inner tapes, we have to acknowledge that our minds function on several layers. In order to avoid mind-boggling technological jargon regarding the layers of the mind, we know we function on a conscious level and on a subconscious level. For simplicity we will keep it on just two layers. The subconscious mind stores our tapes. Think of your mind as a gigantic computer where thousands of informational bits are carefully stored. From learning to walk and to talk to a high school curriculum to our current status in life, and everything in between, information is resting inside of an organ that weighs on an average of three pounds! Our brain has billions of neurons which communicate with one another to keep us daily functioning. The Doctors is a popular television show, and one of the co-hosts, Dr. Travis Stork, says the following about our three pound organ: "Picture 100 billion neurons (or brain cells), which each "fire" (talk to each other) five to 50 times per second (on average). The impulses can travel as fast as 270 miles per hour. This speed is what allows you to see an object (a cat) and immediately identify it."

Just think of all the tapes you and I have stored; it indeed is mind-boggling! Our tapes are very powerful. They can be subtle, uplifting, dynamic, or downright vicious. Their power can be mightier than the worst of hurricanes and faster than Superman himself. They have the power to change our thoughts, emotions, and behavior in a split second. So, what exactly are these invisible powerhouses we call "tapes"? Can they really be life changing?

As a homework assignment, I asked one of my clients to list all the negative tapes that she could recall being told as a youth. Here are just a few that she remembered:

"You're costing me too much."
"Your friends are no good, and you're gonna be just like them."
"Worldly things are evil."
"You should be at church every time the doors are open."
"Sex is wrong."
"Education is a waste, and God is not in education."
"Sex is shameful and dirty and not for discussion."
"Every family has an ugly duckling and you're it."
"You can't do anything without me."
"The devil will get you."
"Children born outside marriage are outcasts."

Have you been told any of these? The tragedy is that this client is only in her thirties! Imagine living forty more years with these tapes dominating one's mind?

At any point in time, our tapes are running in a positive or negative way. They are giving us messages that we may have heard when we were young, or when we are adults. Usually the "adult tapes" can be evaluated, categorized, and understood without too much of a hassle

As for the "child tapes" they can be more of a challenge. When we heard them for the first time, we may not have reached the age in which we were able to process them in a successful manner. They may have been based on the reactions of others towards us while we were still kids, children, or teenagers. The tapes that are negative in their message can be self-destructive, chaotic, and stressful.

Let's say you go shopping with a good friend. You find a department store that has exactly the dress you have been looking for. You mull over it, ask your friend about it, and no decision can be made because your "child tape" might be sending you a message from your parents from an early age, while shopping with them. *"You don't need that. You are always wanting to spend money. Why can't you be happy with what you have?"* And then instantly your "adult tape" begins its message: *"You have the resources, so purchase it. You deserve a reward for all the things you have done today. Why are you hesitating?"* Talk about a double message. You are being bombarded by conflicting messages. Hopefully, you soon begin to realize what is going on within that three-pound organ. What to do? First of all, don't panic in the department store aisle. It doesn't make for a nice picture. Secondly, take some deep breaths in order to relax. Thirdly, don't make a decision right then about the dress. Return later with a clearer mind. Lastly, maintain your inner power—it allows you to think clearly, act maturely, and feel safely. Go with your inner power. It usually does not steer you wrong.

Positive tapes promote our self-esteem while negative tapes destroy our self-worth. And everybody has tapes! Whether the person telling you the negative message meant it to be intentional or not, the fact is that destructive comments are lodged in our subconscious minds. Depending on which type of tape is playing, (negative or positive), our thoughts, feelings, and actions can be linked to them.

All of us make mistakes due to what is going on in our minds at the time. The mature idea is to personally own our mistakes. Stop blaming others. Be accountable for our own errors. We need to remember that it is those mistakes that have helped shape our meaningful lives into what they are today.

Once we begin examining the negative tapes, then we have a head start on the processing of those tapes. If the tapes happen to be negative, we can expect a certain degree of emotional pain. We will be made aware of the unpleasant messages and situations that have been raining on our parade. The pain that you may feel will be temporary. It will pass. You can count on it. Learn who you are. No-Nonsense learning—stop playing a game with others and with yourself. Learn to be real, to be genuine, to be truthful.

If the tapes happen to be positive, then you will feel the comfort and stability of a worthwhile self-esteem. Your self-image will be wholesome, and your friends will find it delightful to be around you.

His name was Robert. He never ever recalled smiling once he became a teenager. When he began seeing me as a therapist, he was 30. Not a single photo of himself in the family album was of a happy, grinning adolescent. When he was urged to smile or just to grin, his facial expression was more like the grimace of an old man.

Robert had an affluent background. As an entrepreneur, with a master's degree from a renowned state university, he sailed brilliantly into the sea of success. As a family man of twin sons with a seemingly happy marriage of four years, he looked the part of prosperity. Robert was living a successful, self-fulfilling life on the outside. But on the inside was a totally different story.

We first met at a church conference meeting in which I was the guest speaker. A congregation of several hundred interfaith individuals had gathered for the week-end. On several occasions during the three days, his and my paths would cross cordially with a brief salutation. It was on Saturday evening, when the group had a prolonged intermission, that Robert and I chanced upon one another. I ended up listening to one of the most gruesome life stories that I had ever encountered. If I had not been face-to-face with Robert and had not witnessed his ghastly countenance, I would have refused to believe his horrific tale.

Since Robert lived in near proximity to my office, we agreed to begin therapy sessions once our schedules cleared. Three weeks later, his therapeutic journey commenced.

Robert was reared in an affluent gated community. His parents socialized often with those who comprised of the very wealthy echelon in their city. The outward appearance of the family was gregarious-oriented, charities-directed, and benevolent-aimed. Such an appearance gave them a reputation of being phenomenal citizens who deeply cared about those in need. It was all an act, a show. Behind closed doors, life for young Robert was just a day-by-day existence.

The well hidden agenda in Robert's family life was a mom who suffered clinically from paranoid schizophrenia. The days that she did not take her medication resulted in a living nightmare for Robert. If that of his mother's condition was not enough, the father's inability to control his frightful outbursts of intense anger could send chills up one's spine. The anger was unpredictable and horrific to this young boy named Robert. Behind the wealthy ornate front doors, a youthful boy lived in fear, terror, and distress. Because Robert was powerless, he received the blunt of his father's temper and of his mother's bizarre behavior.

Tapes started at the beginning of his life, and Robert became a class-A victim. He was never ever able to remember being told that he was loved or a wonderful joy in the family. He had no recollection of self-enhancing messages from either of his parents. He grew up believing that he was the family liability. His negative tapes of being worthless and unlovable cemented into place over time. His vicious tapes were so powerful that when he eventually heard glowing remarks from teachers, friends, and other relatives, the negative tapes trampled the healthy ones.

Robert lived out his negative tapes. He was able to put forth a pleasing and kind face in public. But inside, he was decaying. He had no idea of how to handle the grotesque messages that he heard day and night. As far as Robert goes now, he made it. However, it did not happen overnight. While there are still times when his negative tapes jump into his conscious mind, he understands their origin and knows how to deal with them on a daily basis.

All of our tapes—positive and negative--are permanent. Some are healthy while others are destructive. The wonderful news is that the negative ones can be re-directed. And the positive ones need to be enhanced and self-promoted on a continual basis.

Make choices that will change your life.

Dr. Ray Ashurst, Ph.D.

Suggestions: Acknowledge that you do have tapes.
If need be, seek out a professional who will help you understand the tapes.
Keep a journal of the tapes and their meanings.
Share your findings with a close friend.
When the pain becomes unbearable, let someone know.
Promote your healthy tapes in every possible way.
Be aware of what you say to your children and friends. They need to hear positive, healthy messages regaarding their self-image.
Stop spreading negative messages to others. Be positive!

Who wants to work all day without some type of reward and recognition? Not me.

CHAPTER 6

NO-NONSENSE REWARDS

Go confidently in the direction of your dreams. Live the life you have imagined.

--Henry David Thoreau

Dedicated to the people in Blairsville, Georgia, and surrounding areas. You have helped me to live life fully. Thank you.

CHAPTER 6

Because we are so busy, we sometimes have a difficult time pursuing our dreams and living life to the fullest. We even manufacture excuses: *"I am too tired." "I don't deserve it." "What would people think?" "I'll do it later in life."* So many of us have a hard time rewarding ourselves. Isn't it strange that as intellectual human beings we are more prone to reward our pets for good deeds rather than ourselves? Very mystifying. Whenever our lovable pets do what we want or just show us unconditional affection, we offer them lots of treats from the goodie bag. Not just once a day but countless times daily if your pets are like mine. Do I really spoil my three cats: Sylvester, Precious, Tigger, and two dogs: Ivy, and Scooter? Yep! Guilty as charged. And if you have pets as part of your family, don't tell me you aren't the same. They need rewards, and thus we give them. After all, they are intricate parts of our family circle. Then why are we more apt to reward our pets than ourselves?

Bestowing rewards is just not limited to our pets. If you have children, then handing out rewards is natural, automatic, and healthy. Providing rewards is our way to let children know that as parents, we are pleased with their specific behaviors, positive attitudes, and mannerisms. The basis for giving rewards is sometimes not just limited to their good deeds. We do it to remind them that they are loved, admired, and appreciated.

However, what rewards do we give ourselves? We are used to being tenderhearted to children, family members, friends, and pets, and yet we forget a very important person—ourselves. If the truth be known, we seldom give ourselves worthy rewards, or for that matter, any rewards. The reason may be because we feel guilty, unworthy, self-pity, martyrdom, or only Heaven knows why, we just don't. We fail to realize that by our neglect of rewarding ourselves, our self-worth and self-esteem can become damaged. We are not feeding ourselves healthy, wonderful acclamations in life. Whether the rewards are for something we have accomplished or for someone whom we have helped, we deserve the self-recognition. The recognition may not come from another person, but it still needs to come even if we are the ones ourselves who do it.

We are worthy to be recognized for all the responsibilities we do day-in and day-out.

****

The reward of a thing well done is to have done it.

--Ralph Waldo Emerson

****

Let's face it: we may be the only one who even recognizes our daily accomplishments. Thus, it is necessary that we understand this concept: *rewards promote self-worth.* Each time we pat ourselves on the back, we are congratulating our self-esteem. It is actually enhanced. God instructs us to think highly of ourselves, to love ourselves, and to love others.

"Thou shalt love thy neighbor as thyself" – James 2:8

We all live a very rushed life, and it can often times become hectic and stressful. We may not be free to reward ourselves during the day or evening after each of our achievements. We may have to wait until we have accomplished several tasks before rewarding ourselves. Our simple prayer may be, *"Lord, thank you today for allowing me to do the wash, for putting away the dishes, for vacuuming the house, and for paying our bills."* Such achievements are not going to stop traffic or move mountains, but they are tasks nevertheless that must be done. Even accomplishing simple things deserves our attention and rewards. Each single one of our finished tasks deserves a worthwhile reward. But to stop to do each reward individually may not be possible, so combining them can be just as effective. And then another prayer can be given: *"I am rewarding myself because of the things that I have accomplished these past few days. Thank you, Lord, for letting me feel good about myself."*

As a result, you have taken the time to bathe your self-worth in a wonderful way. You can even feel the positive impact. And this process of rewarding yourself is continuous. Each day at home, at work, at school, and wherever you plant your feet, you will have opportunities to accomplish many valuable tasks and as a result, reward yourself multiple times. Depending on how you evaluate each task, you are to determine the reward. You may feel that a certain task is worth an ice cream cone while another deserves a nice restaurant meal, extra time to read a book, or watch a favorite television program. This goes for the man or woman. Each deserves a reward to accomplished duties. You are the one to decide on what tasks deserve what rewards. At first, this Life Skill may feel quite strange because we have never taken the time or opportunity to be good to ourselves. So prepare yourself for some wonderful moments after you begin applying this Skill and say farewell to a lot of stress.

During the years I have been a therapist, I have encountered many individuals who have never applied this Life Skill for one reason or the other. The client whom I have in mind was the antithesis of utilizing the reward system. She had been taught all of her life that her duty was to maintain a clean, neat, efficient, and organized home. This was expected of her, and she did it in fine style. Because it was expected, she was programmed not to give herself any pats on the back. She grew up believing that a manicured house appearance was her job and that such a fine appearance was certainly reward enough.

From her preadolescence, Brandy was saddled with performing specific home responsibilities. A small amount was at the beginning, such as washing the dishes, setting the table, and vacuuming the house. As she matured, so did her duties: planning the evening meals and cooking them, household shopping, and babysitting her young siblings. And in time her responsibilities increased to a monstrous level. And still she never rewarded herself because of the mind-manipulation from her parents.

For sure, all children in a family need daily chores once they reach an age in which responsibilities can be administered and transacted. The sadness with Brandy lies not in her assigned duties but rather in her not being given the freedom to reward herself for her deeds of accomplishment.

When the time came that Brandy had her own home with a husband and three children, she was well prepared for taking charge. She continued to carry forth her home responsibilities with absolutely no self-rewards. Her mind had been explicitly programmed that she did not deserve any praise because her reward was in doing her duties as a loving wife and mother.

When I met Brandy for our first session, she looked as if she had been run over by a powerful riding lawnmower. Her hair was disheveled, her face had a sunken appearance, and her clothes looked worn. She was a very tired person. Her reason for seeing me was a referral from a local physician.

As our conversations developed into months, her significant problems related to her self-worth which was at a critical low. She knew that she was being taken for granted. And she felt like a throw rug on which her family walked and at times cleaned the dirt off their shoes. Brandy was beaten down and completely exhausted physically, emotionally, and mentally.

For a woman in just her twenties, she was living a defeated life with no enjoyment or fulfillment. After a few sessions, I determined that (1) she had never given herself any worthwhile rewards for accomplished tasks, (2) she expected herself to be "mighty woman" day-in and day-out, and (3) she was at the mercy of all those occupying her home. When I asked Brandy what type of rewards did she give herself after completing her chores, she responded in an eerie way: her face registered confusion, her body stiffened, her laugh was sinister. Her tears were heart-breaking. She actually had no idea what I meant by rewards.

Before the reward system could become a reality for Brandy, we had to address her anger towards her family members. Her hostility was deep and unforgiving. So, sessions upon sessions were dedicated to resolving her emotional roadblocks.

Changing habits is not an easy assignment. It takes work and plenty of courage, dedication, and commitment. Since Brandy had never given herself any type of rewards based on her daily accomplishments, this habit was entrenched in her lifestyle. In addition, it never crossed her mind that she was entitled to receive anything for doing what she was told was her role in life.

Therefore, it was like a foreign language to her when we talked about the reward system. At first, it wasn't natural for Brandy to accept the dynamics of this Life Skill. She just could not wrap her mind around the idea of celebrating her tasks with rewards. She felt unworthy of any recognition for her daily efforts. During one of our sessions, she actually broke out laughing at the mere thought of giving herself rewards. It was as if she had never realized the importance of her work and of herself.

Brandy suffered from a syndrome of "the woman doing all she can do to make each family member happy and satisfied." Brandy had seldom received any pats on the back from anyone in her immediate family, and when she did, the compliments were infinitesimal in scope. She received plenty of criticism, but very little praise to speak of. As a result, for many years, she did not have a support system to build up a positive self-worth.

My treatment plan for Brandy seemed self- evident. Her self-image needed an overhaul. And such a treatment can become most difficult because it involves the subconscious mind. The subconscious part of our brain is highly stubborn. It hates to change because it has been used to doing things the same way indefinitely. It defies us to challenge it with any intent of changing it. For example, each morning we all have a pattern of behavior: For some of you, brushing your teeth, showering, and then getting dressed is the scheme. The same way every single day. The subconscious is accustomed to that behavioral pattern. But if we change that order of behavior and take a shower before brushing our teeth, or getting dressed before brushing, our behavior will feel weird. Try it. We will have thrown a fast curve ball at our unexpected subconscious. The same was for Brandy. She was used to performing her household duties without any personal self-recognition.

However, the good news is that the stubborn subconscious mind can change. When the conscious mind continues to instruct the subconscious with a particular message, over time the subconscious is obliged to change...but not without a fight. But alas! It is worth it.

With Brandy, she had to be convinced that she was worthy of the reward system. Then next she was assigned to begin giving herself rewards after she completed her tasks. For example, once she vacuumed, she got an extra 30 minutes to read her book at night. When she did the family laundry, she rewarded herself by watching an hour of her favorite afternoon television show.

With repetitious commands to her subconscious, Brandy was able to finally accept self-awards without cringing. Her self-worth went through a remarkable transformation over time. Her self-image took on the genuine appearance of a confident, assertive, self-actualizing individual, both within the family household and with her relatives, friends, and community acquaintances.

Behavior patterns can definitely be instructed to change from the negative to the positive. It is a thrilling experience to witness it in oneself. However, it does require the individual to recognize and to admit one's negative behavior pattern as being detrimental and faulty.

And next it requires an honest desire to want to change to a positive, comfortable, and acceptable pattern of behavior.

Before any desired change can occur, the individual must find it necessary and worthwhile to stop the present negative behavior. We can always use the command **Stop** to what we have been doing.

Stand
Tall
On
Principles

You are only one step away from changing your life.

Suggestions: *Keep a small notebook to daily record your accomplishments.*
Check off each task for which you have given yourself a reward.
Decide what your reward will be before beginning the task.
Tell a friend about your plan of rewards. Ask that person to hold you accountable.
Ask your friend to be a partner and do the same reward system.
*You can begin your reward system **now**.*

The next chapter deals with absolute truth.
Truth can create or destroy your happiness.

CHAPTER 7

NO-NONSENSE TRUTHFULNESS

The only measure of what you believe is what you do. If you want to know what people believe, don't read what they write, don't ask them what they believe, just observe what they do.

--Ashley Montagu

Dedicated to the people at Dale City Baptist Church who believed in what God was doing with the Youth Program.

CHAPTER 7

Small deeds done are better
than great deeds planned.

--Peter Marshall

You and I are bombarded hourly by words, more words, and even more words. Day-by-day we are caught in the middle of verbiage, never ending. Even our friends and family members are entering into our sandbox (space) continually with words and expressions that we have to process. We try to escape, but wherever we go, we run into some type of communication asking us to do something, to go somewhere, or to be someone in particular. Cell phones, land phones, computers, televisions, and voices are ever-present.

Words are basically inexpensive, unless you are talking to a lawyer or therapist. While words may sound nice, such as *"You are my friend forever,"* or *"I'll do anything for you"*--these are just mere words and nothing more as far as the real truth can be discerned.

On the market, words are cheap with no commitments attached.

Words can get to the point that they become exhausting. In ages past, people did put their trust in another person's word with simply a handshake. Those days are long gone.

The closest thing to the absolute truth is actions, one's behavior. Why? Everything we do has a purpose—washing, cleaning, cooking, shopping, eating-- everything we do has a reason for being done. So, if we want to know the truth, observe a person's behavior. If we want to really, really know the truth about the personality of someone, take a look at that individual's daily actions.

As a reader, are you old enough to remember those Sunday automobile drives with our parents? They would pile us in our family vehicle and away we would go on a Sunday exploration. No particular destination. No exact time limit. And absolutely no fussing and fighting. The action was to go somewhere with the family, and that action became the truth of our experiencing an exciting Sunday journey together.

If somebody tells you that your lawn will be mowed within a few days, you still shouldn't be waiting, waiting a month later. As the saying goes, *"The proof is in the pudding."* And then when we see that person in public, the individual may go overboard offering all types of excuses for not showing up. His lack of action prosecutes himself. Duh! Get yourself a more reliable and truthful gardener.

> *If we find ourselves acting out behaviors*
> *we thought unthinkable,*
> *then therein is an element of truth.*

When one examines the life of Jesus Christ, His words are always backed up by His actions.

> *"God anointed Jesus of Nazareth with the Holy Spirit, and with power; who went about doing good, and healing all that were oppressed of the devil; for God was with Him." – Acts 10:38*

As human beings, at times we don't always do what we say we will do. We might intend to follow through on what we say, but truthfully it's only words and good intentions. However, from time-to-time, we do meet a person whose word is gold—that individual does what is promised. Such a person is valuable to know--the individual's honesty, integrity, and dependability are trademarks.

> *"This above all: to thine own self be true,*
> *And it must follow, as the night the day,*
> *Thou canst not then be false to any man."*
>
> *--Shakespeare, <u>Hamlet</u>*

****

Honesty is the first chapter in the book of wisdom.

--Thomas Jefferson

****

Most of us would probably like having such a persona, but for one reason or another, we just will not always do what we promise. We may mean it at the time. However, each time we fail to uphold our promises with actions, then our self-image takes a direct hit.

This Life Skill of doing what we promise brings honor to our Creator and to ourselves. In addition, it just feels good when we carry out our word. It is easy sometimes to put our mouths in action before we place our brains in gear. After we have given our word, we may then have second thoughts. And with those thoughts, we may forfeit our promises. We do a lot of promising because words are easily spit out. However, supporting those words with actions can be the challenge.

One of the greatest compliments that you and I can ever receive is being told that someone can "take our word to the bank." *"I will do what I say. You can count on it."* Such statements mean that we possess in us the truest form of pure integrity and honesty. We spend much time promising what we think we are supposed to promise and saying what we believe people want to hear. Unfortunately, those intended promises fall under a suffocating blanket of deceit and untruth.

The No-Nonsense of truthfulness means doing exactly what we say we will do. No excuses. No backing out. No blaming. Fulfill your promises in order to have a remarkable reputation of a truthful, reliable, dependable person. The real truth is not in us if our tongues say one thing and our feet say another. This type of Non-Nonsense Life Skill will definitely help to reduce your stress level. Simply do what you say. Being trustworthy promotes our self-esteem, and any way we can find to zap our stress needs to be done.

Dismissing a client was by far the hardest professional task that I ever had to do as a therapist. The decision was gut-wrenching, but I knew it was definitely required of me. If I were to remain honest with myself and to retain my integrity to any degree, I had a responsibility to the client and to my myself.

A cardinal principle in therapeutic situations is the necessity of the client to be as truthful as humanly possible if any measure of success is to be accomplished. If the truth isn't told, then time is a waste. It does take time before the client is comfortable with the therapist, but honesty must prevail if there is to be creditability in the relationship.

Eric was thirty-five when he began his personal journey on the therapeutic road with me. He presented himself as a well-groomed, bright gentleman who was keenly interested and fascinated with the dynamics of learning who he was. On many occasions he would bring self-help books to his sessions in order to inquire how certain principles could possibly fit into his life. *(Since you are presently holding a self-help book, I couldn't very well forbid him to read them.)*

Eric had an inquisitive personality. There were times when he would come across more like an academic student than as a searching client. In the beginning, our sessions were both enlightening and entertaining, if therapy sessions can rightly be labeled as such. He never became a "know-it-all" or a fanatic searcher on his journey. He would listen to my insights and challenges.

I am not certain at what point on Eric's journey that his 2 + 2 did not equal 4. Maybe it was simply my gut feeling or perhaps an acute awareness that caused me to question his "truths" extremely close. His details didn't compute, his feelings seemed questionable, and his random thoughts were without any validity. Rather than point an invisible, accusing finger at Eric, I chose to examine myself first.

Having a psychologist friend nearby was not only a luxury but a salvation. I had many questions that dealt with the manner in how Eric's therapy was being conducted. Was I being judgmental or accusing? Sarcastic or straight-forward? Condemning or accepting? Multiple discussions with my friend had to be held so that I could exonerate myself and continue my sessions with Eric.

The mind-set I had with Eric was my doubting his honesty and his desire to even be near truthful. I think that I really wanted to believe him, but the discrepancy between what he claimed as truth and what he actually did was as wide as the east from the west.

Eric claimed he was committed to his therapy, but yet he missed more appointments in a month than he attended. Eric proclaimed he was earning a graduate degree which occupied his time, and yet I found out that he was dismissed from the school due to failing grades and a lack of attendance. According to Eric, he maintained an immaculate home with expensive furnishings. However, upon my visit to his house, I found it in shambles and what furnishings there were, he would not have had any bragging rights.

The lack of truth totaled more than Pinocchio's nose could have withstood. So, the question and answer I had to face was to what degree of stamina did I have in dealing with a perpetual truth-stretcher. How much energy would it require to maintain the sessions? For Eric's sake, would it be better to refer him to a psychological specialist?

As a therapist, there are occasions when one has to admit that one does not have the needed answers and necessary training. We simply just may not know the solutions. It can be difficult to admit and to face. However, if one is to adhere to the truth, then being honest with self is essential and with the client.

I have come to terms with dismissing Eric as a client. It doesn't keep me awake at nights or stressed during the day. The ultimate honesty in this situation was to admit to self that someone else could hopefully do a more effective job for Eric's sake. I never found out whether he contacted the specialist or decided to face life on his own terms.

We each have the power to require those in our space to be fair, honest, kind, and truthful. If a person can't meet such basic requirements, then we have the right to **STOP** providing space for them in our scheduled agenda.

Stand
Tall
On
Principles

Remember: *You are only one moment away from changing your life.*

Suggestions: *We may need professional help to undo the mental cobwebs of our untruths towards others.*

Find someone whom you trust explicitly to hold you accountable for your promises. Ask your friend to hold your feet to the fire.

Begin a new life philosophy: "Do what I say I will do." Reward yourself when you fulfill your promise.

Ask God to convict you about your promises. He is great at this!

Apologize to those individuals whom you have not kept your word.

Want to feel good about yourself?
Be careful whom you ask.

CHAPTER 8

NO-NONSENSE SELF-ESTEEM

*No one can make you feel inferior
without your consent.*

--Eleanor Roosevelt

*Dedicated to my brother, Ed, Jr.,
and his wife, Sherry.
Also to my nephew Ed, III.
And to my niece Robin and her
husband, Duane.
And to my niece Amy and her husband, Ryan.
They are a joy to know.*

CHAPTER 8

How do you see yourself? How much value do you place on your self-worth? The answers to these questions are crucial. They will indicate whether you view yourself highly or otherwise. What and how we see ourselves also will determine our lifestyle. Our self-esteem will be portrayed in our family life as well as in our social surroundings. We cannot detach ourselves from our self-esteem. It goes wherever we go.

We can be strange creatures at times. We measure ourselves by what people say and think about us. It is usually the important individuals in our lives who help in shaping our self-image or assist in destroying it—our family members, friends, teachers, and even coworkers. These individuals play a significant role in the way we view our worthiness and value. Furthermore, we also gear our physical appearance on what others think. We tend to give people our ultimate power, and unfortunately at times, our self-worth gets an exhaustive workout.

Our self-esteem begins at birth and is shaped by those around us. How we feel about ourselves guides our emotions, thoughts, and actions. If our self-esteem is positive, then we feel internal satisfaction on a daily basis. Daily problems are handled properly, and with our positive self-esteem, we are able to recognize, evaluate, and solve problems in a healthy way.

However, a person with poor self-esteem has a down-trodden mind, and solving daily problems is a chore. One's self-picture is poor. Living life becomes morose and depressive. If we grow up thinking and being told that we are unworthy, then we conduct ourselves as being useless. We actually believe the messages. They have become cemented in our minds. As a result, we drag ourselves around throughout the day.

****

Trust God. You are exactly where you are meant to be.

--Hallmark

****

God tells us that we become what we think:

"For as he thinks in his heart, so is he." – *Proverbs 23:7*

God does not want us to live defeated lives but rather an abundant life in Him:

"And the grace of our Lord gives exceedingly abundant with faith and love which is in Christ Jesus." *I Timothy 1:14*

We can change our poor self-image into a vibrant, positive one. It is not an impossibility.

The sad realization for those with a damaged self-esteem is knowing that some of the messages came from one's own family members. It may not have been intentional, but it did happen. And we often swallowed the negative comments hook, line, and sinker. How tragic! Even if the comments were made in a joking manner while we were at a tender age, we did not have at the time the capacity to reason what was and what wasn't. We may have heard that we were lazy, stupid, and crazy. Those destructive remarks, known as tapes, planted themselves into our minds, and because we believed them, we might still be paying the price as adults. A wounded self-esteem will always be a highly frustrating one. Rather than having confidence and stability, we live in despair and sadness.

A wounded self-esteem can create daily frustrations and doubts. There is a lack of security and trust within oneself to handle day-by-day situations effectively. Our thought-processing is tainted with a low self-image, and as a result, we don't feel comfortable and secure in making simple decisions. With a negative self-image, just managing to survive in our unpredictable, global society, constitutes a daily challenge. Some days we may win and other days, not so well.

With a positive self-esteem, our outlook perpetuates itself with a genuine happiness and contentment. The profound truth is that we are what we think. Think positive, be positive.

"For as he thinketh in his heart, so is he." – Proverbs 23:8

God says it so plainly: we feel the way we do because of the thoughts we think. Our healthy self-esteem is based on a positive image reflecting in our life mirror. Thinking and acting in a positive way determines how we will handle all types of circumstances in our daily lives. Continual healthy thinking, plus believing in oneself, produces a remarkable self-esteem and self-image.

****

"It takes courage to grow up and become who you really are.

--E. E. Cummings

****

Be ye transformed by the renewing of your mind (our thinking), that ye may prove what is that good, and acceptable, and perfect will of God." – Romans 12:2

The renewing of one's mind offers wonderful hope to those shackled with a destructive self-esteem. A secure confidence can be ours. The mind renewing itself in a positive way is a daily challenge and objective. In our secular society, there are human forces that tempt us to abandon at times our spiritual ideals and positive self-image. It sometimes becomes difficult to maintain healthy and worthwhile thinking. Renewing one's mind can enhance a positive self-esteem. The benefit of maintaining a healthy self-esteem is inner peace and contentment. Pure happiness is available, and God is always ready to make it happen for us.

****

Happiness is not a state to arrive at, but a manner of traveling.

--Samuel Johnson

****

Truthfully we know who we are. All of us are filled with limitations and struggles, but when we handle those conflicts in a healthy manner, our positive self-worth is enhanced. We always will have life trials, heartaches, and tribulations attempting to beat down our mental and emotional doors. We live in a horrifying world. However, our comfort and ability in dealing with such challenges come from the confidence we have in ourselves and from the faith we have in God. He will guide us safely through troubled waters:

"God will keep us in perfect peace, when our mind stays on God and His Word; because we trust in God." – Isaiah 26:3

There will be days when our get-up-and-go has got-up-and-went. Our energy level and enthusiasm are drained absolutely dry. However, we still can utilize our positive self-worth. It cannot be destroyed or diminished unless we allow it. It is based on what we know about ourselves, not on what others think.

Our thought patterns can empower us in a strengthening way. Rather than allowing life situations to bend us to look like a pretzel, our attention needs to center on knowing who we are and what we are capable of.

Our Creator, in eternity past, knew that you and I would have problematic situations during our lifetime; thus, He gave us the spirit of power, love, and a sound mind.

"For God hath not given us the spirit of fear, but of power, and of love, and of a sound mind."
--I Timothy 1:7

Whatever traumatic situations we face daily can be handled effectively as human and spiritual beings. The situations may not end up the way we want, but we can still keep intact our integrity and dignity. Maintaining a healthy self-esteem, self-image, and self-worth will enable a person to "get up again" after he has been "beaten down."

Sometimes the human will in us may wish to tangle with those individuals who are creating havoc in our lives and who are attempting to destroy our self-image. However, we are instructed to leave that person to God:

> *"Judge not, that you be not judged. For with what judgment you judge, you will be judged; and with the measure you use, it will be measured back to you" – Matthew 7:1-2*

> ***Get on with your life. Don't look over your shoulder. Eyes and feet straight ahead. God has your back.***

****

Love yourself first and everything else falls into line.

--Lucille Ball

****

We are not here by accident during this specific time-line in history.

A man and wife were flying above a much traveled highway. Suddenly the wife gasped and pointed to a car passing another on a hill. *"There's another car coming on the other side. The driver passing can't see it."* As she covered her face in horror, the husband-pilot grimly remarked, *"Now we know how God feels."* God has planted a purpose in our lives. We just need to see it.

Different people=Different purpose.

As we search out our purpose, we can begin seeing and understanding the reason for our being here during this century. We are not guaranteed that stress will not be a part of our lives. Stress is part of life. The thing is to remember that we are not here on earth as a fluke, without purpose and meaning. Combine such a purpose with a healthy self-esteem, and therefore we can become a dynamic, positive force on earth, living out our purpose. When Thomas A. Edison thought he had discovered the way to record and to reproduce the sound of a human voice on a machine, he called in a model maker. Handing the man a rough pencil sketch of his idea, he asked that a working model be built. The model maker surveyed the sketch, then declared, *"Impossible. That thing will never work." "What makes you think it won't work?"* Edison asked. *"Because no one has ever made a machine that could talk,"* the model maker exclaimed. Instead of accepting this verdict, Edison determinedly said, *"Build what I have sketched here and let me be the loser if it doesn't work."* (Dictionary of Illustrations) Edison had confidence in himself. All of us have the same opportunity each day—believing in our self-worth which leads to an amazing self-confidence.

The question we must answer is how to define ourselves. How do we see our meaning in life? If we define ourselves with a low self-worth, then our continual efforts will be futile—a confused purpose with an obscure meaning. On the other hand, if we define ourselves with a foundation of a healthy self-esteem, then our style of living each day will be exciting, adventuresome, and plain fun even in the midst of a stressful day. We might not smile all day, but we know where the smile comes from.

****

People are just about as happy as they make up their minds to be.

--Abraham Lincoln

****

Our motto surely can be:

Stand aside, world. Here I come.

There will be times when we are worked to a frazzle, emotionally spent, and weak as a kitten, but yet we can thrive due to our fortitude, our heightened self-esteem, plus our faith in our Creator who knows every single thing we are facing.

Making spiritual choices will change your life abundantly.

Suggestions: Solutions to problems are "do-able" if you are grounded.

If a poor self-esteem occupies your inner self, get professional help.

Take time to pray that your positive self-esteem will be protected.

Associate with those who have a positive self-image.

List 10 affirmations about yourself and then have a friend read them back to you.

Read books that will enhance your self-esteem, self-image, self-worth

Sometimes we are stressed over making correct day-by-day decisions.

The next chapter can free you from such anxiety.

CHAPTER 9

NO-NONSENSE DECISION MAKING

Just don't give up trying to do what you really want to do. Where there is love and inspiration, I don't think you can go wrong.

---Ella Fitzgerald

Dedicated to my 1962 classmates at St. Petersburg High School who cared enough about me to be my friends and to help me with so many decisions.

Thanks.

CHAPTER 9

We make dozens of decisions hourly. Trying to make effective decisions that are part of our hour-by-hour issues sometimes can be totally overwhelming. It's not unusual that we question our own thought processing. *"Am I doing justice to each decision?" "Have I thought through each decision carefully?"* Whether the issues are small or large, each requires a mature call on our part. From selecting a movie that the entire family will enjoy watching to picking the paint colors that will enhance the beauty of our home, our decision-making process means "living" with our final choices. Our decisions require us to utilize our judgment abilities. At times our brains seem to be screaming out "HELP"--and now!

There are **no** wrong decisions in life! Shocked? We have been conditioned all of our lives that decisions we make are either good or bad. The decisions that I am referring to are **not** those concerning our ethical, moral, spiritual decisions. Those decisions definitely have a "good or bad" attached to them. The focused decisions in which this chapter deals are those day-by-day mundane decisions that we all have to make.

We at times make crazy decisions and wonder what we were thinking. And in so many circumstances, those daily decisions can add unbelievable stress in our lives.

Shakespeare's <u>Merchant of Venice</u> contains a memorable scene suggesting the perils of decision-making. In choosing among three swains, Portia takes a gold locket from her neck and places it in one of the three caskets; one is made of gold, another of silver, and the last is lead. The Prince of Morocco reads the engraving on the gold casket: *"Who chooseth me shall gain what many men desire."* He chooses the gold box and finds it empty. The Prince of Arragon takes the silver casket, on which is inscribed, *"Who chooseth me shall get as much as he deserves."* He also finds it empty. Finally, Bassanio selects the lead box on which is written, *"Who chooseth me must give and hazard all he hath."* Inside he finds the gold locket which is the key to Portia's heart. (Dictionary of Illustrations)

Decision-making can be mind-boggling when one thinks of all the decisions that we make in just one day. Hundreds and hundreds, from the time we rise until the ending of our day. We are all going to make questionable decisions as we journey through life. Some decisions are made in which we beat up ourselves while others put a smile on our faces.

We tend to lump all of our decision-making into one pile: the everyday decisions and the moral and ethical decisions. When we do such a thing, we manufacture a monumental destructive mind-structure. The two types of decisions are as different as night and day. There is a huge difference in making daily mundane decisions and in making decisions that involve our spiritual and moral teachings. We have to differentiate day-by-day mundane decisions, such as what food to purchase or which pair of shoes to wear, from the decisions relating to our personal belief system. Not making a dividing line between the two types of decision-making will create confusion, stress, and frustration.

Because we are used to thinking daily decisions are either correct or not, we spend much of our time either celebrating or lamenting. The truth of the matter is that daily decisions do not have personalities.

They are inanimate. They can't think. They are simply decisions—no right, no wrong. They are just good-ole, homespun decisions. Nothing more, nothing less. Some decisions that we make on a daily basis may result in being effective ones while others are not. This is a learning process.

On any given afternoon, you are trying to locate an address in the community in which you live. You feel yourself becoming flustered because you aren't sure the correct way to your destination. Finally, you come near to your arrival scene. However, you are faced with a split in the road. You have no idea whether to go left or right. (and you don't have a GPS system) So, you try right. After your arrival, you find out that it took you 30 minutes longer than if you had chosen the left one. Was you decision bad or wrong? No, no, no. It was just a decision. In and of themselves, decisions do not have power. You learned that a more effective way of getting to your destination the next time is to go right, not left. This is the learning process.

Another experience we can all identify with is shopping for groceries. You have guests coming to supper. You are standing in front of multiple spaghetti sauces. You decide to select a new brand that has just come on the market. The guests arrive, salads are served, and time for the main meal. You realize that no one is bragging on your spaghetti like they normally do. Then you taste it. You realize it doesn't have your magic taste. Were you wrong in selecting a new sauce brand? No, no, no. It simply wasn't the most effective decision.

Once you have grabbed hold of this Life Skill, your decision-making will become healthier and easier on your nerves. The idea is to maintain our stress level which means we must look at daily decisions as effective ones or not. We become less stressed when we view these types of decisions as no big deal! They are just decisions. We learn from the ineffective ones and smile at the effective ones.

The other category of decision-making involves our belief system—our moral, ethical, and spiritual background. Being human means that we have occasionally made decisions that have gone contrary to what we morally and ethically believe. These types of decisions are not easily dismissed in our minds, unlike the daily mundane decisions. When decisions are made that conflict with our personal belief system, our mind is receiving mixed messages, thus creating stress and chaos. On one hand, our mind has already integrated a belief system into our very essence—our self-esteem, our self-worth, our self-image. Then it has to process a new message involving our behavior that is opposite of those beliefs. Like a computer, the mind is not certain what it is to do with the mixed messages. It waits for us to clear up the confusion in order that it can return to its normal functioning.

Being humans, we will at times do things that are destructive. We make mistakes.

How often when we blunder, and are filled with guilty shame,
Do we invent excuses, and attempt to shift the blame!
But when we make mistakes, I find it's sensible and wise
To honestly admit them, and omit the alibis.

--Mary Hamlett Goodman

One of my favorite Bible teachers says, *"When the smoke clears, if we are alive, then God still has a purpose for our lives."*

Even with all the crazy, mundane decisions
that we make, they are not fatal.

Since 1914 framed placards with the word **Think** have been on the walls of offices and plants of the IBM Corporations all over the world. The one-word challenge was initiated by IBM founder, Thomas Watson, Sr. Mr. Watson was well known for his aggressive integrity learned from his devout Methodist father. He also gained a reputation as "the world's greatest salesman," and for saying, *"The trouble with every one of us is that we don't think enough. We don't get paid for working with our feet—we get paid for working with our head."* (Dictionary of Illustrations)

****

Two roads diverged in a wood, and
I took the one less traveled by,
And that has made all the difference.

--Robert Frost

****

One of the sweetest and kindest clients I have ever had was a frail-looking sixty-one year old, true Southern lady. She insisted that I call her by her nickname, Miss Lily. One couldn't help lovin' Miss Lily. In all of our sessions, she never belittled anyone or placed blame on any person other than herself. She dressed immaculately and came prepared for each session with her 5x3 notepad and a local bank's complimentary pen—and she made sure each session that I knew she did not freely "lift" the pen but that it was a gift.

When an individual reaches 61, the assumption could be argued that such a person has already dealt with the more serious conflicts in one's life, or a 61 year-old person has no desire to hang out one's "dirty laundry of problems" to a stranger. Plus, the belief is that anyone over the age of 61 has better things to do with one's time and money than seeing a therapist.

Miss Lily had no intentions of wasting her time and mine and of "dedicating" her funds to therapy over a long period of time. Within a few times together, Miss Lily had her cards on the "therapy table" to be discussed, analyzed, and solved, as Miss Lily aptly stated it.

Miss Lily struggled with the challenges of making decisions. This struggle has been lifelong, and at 61, she finally made up her mind to advance towards a solution. She had not learned to differentiate between decisions involving her value system and those dealing with the everyday, mundane ones. In her mind, all decisions were equal-based, equal-important, and equal-stressful. No wonder Miss Lily's internal world resembled that of a manufactured pretzel. Her desire of making the right choice regarding everyday mundane decisions was intermingled with awful confusion, frightful dread, and at times horrendous guilt. She believed that her decisions had to be 100% accurate and correct. One can only imagine the misery of such a life, worrying if her choice in a particular brand of bread was perfect to match the family meal that evening.

As for my diagnosis of her situation, it was immediate and turned out to be right on the mark. In my treatment plan it was necessary that Miss Lily be re-programmed regarding decision-making. She had to accept that not every decision that she made in her life had to end up being stressful, intense, and earth-shattering. Re-regulating her mind-set required that she develop a crystal clear understanding of the difference between the routine, day-to-day decisions and the moral and ethical ones that guided and inspired her.

It was important and comforting to Miss Lily that her religious standards involving her moral and ethical lifestyle were not up for grabs during her therapy sessions. Such matters were not on the "therapy table" to be hassled over or to be vigorously dismantled unless she desired to address such specific issues. This proclamation indeed pleased Miss Lily.

The real therapeutic work for this pleasant-minded 61 year-old was accepting that her normal daily decisions were not life-threatening or self-destructive. They were simply decisions—not bad, not good, **but rather** effective or ineffective. If the drinks she selected did not go with the evening meal, no big deal! It was just a decision. It wasn't a bad choice but just not an effective one. That's all! The next day the mountains would be still in place, the streams would continue to flow, and the interstate traffic would be still annoying. In other words, Miss Lilly's particular drink selection did not call forth an emergency meeting of the United Nations.

The error that we make, along with Miss Lily, is feeling that each day we must label our workaday decisions as good or bad ones. By doing so, we set up ourselves to be miserable for the remainder of the day. And let's face it: after a couple of decisions that we have labeled as bad, we are down and out for the count. And there are times when we carry those burdensome decisions into the next day and the next and the next.

Rather than wandering around in the "Fretful Field" all day regarding decisions that you have made, you can relax much easier and enjoy the day more by stop condemning yourself and your decisions.

We have the ability to **STOP** beating up ourselves by simply remembering that not all decisions are going to be effective nor ineffective. It's the way life goes. Enjoy your day. Find something refreshing to do. And then go do it.

Stand

Tall

On

Principles

You are only one step away from changing your life.

Suggestions: *Thank God each day that you are still alive.*
Be alert to your own actions, comments, and decisions.
Share the history of your life with others.
Decisions can be changed.
Stop labeling your decisions "good or bad".

It is very, very important to remember that decisions which involve one's value system can be right or wrong! Be aware that you distinguish between those, and those we make which have no moral consequences!

All of us have some type of problems, and the challenge is to figure out which ones are really ours. This will require your own self analysis.

CHAPTER 10

NO-NONSENSE PROBLEMS

If you're not doing what you
need to do, why not?

--Gary Pennell

Dedicated to my lifelong friends
for helping me to determine which
problems belong to others.

CHAPTER 10

Tit-for-tat: You did it. No, you did it. No, you did. And it goes on and on and on. No conclusion is reached since the involved participants trust in their own individual discernment. Whoever really is at fault in the situation remains dormant because of the tit-for-tat game. And so we live our lives in futile attempts of proving ourselves to be the innocent one, and the other person is at fault. Our energy level becomes exhaustive, and usually no one is determined right or wrong. The situation is like a seesaw—up, down, up, down—no one gives in.

So similar to the tit-for-tat round is our being caught up in disagreements involving our friends and family members. By choice or invitation we become engaged in conflicts that can involve a few folks to many. The conflicts can seemingly take our breath away due to the uproar and emotional punches. At a certain point we may wonder how in the world did we even become involved? And mercy, how do we escape on reasonable terms? At times we are not sure what to do.

A sad looking character was shown into the office of a prominent psychiatrist. *"I've lost all desire to go on, doctor. Life has become too hectic, too confused."* *"Yes,"* said the doctor, clucking sympathetically. *"I understand. We all have our problems. You'll need a year or two of treatments at one hundred dollars a session."* There was a pause. *"Well, that solves your problem, Doc. Now what about mine?"* (Eleanor Doan)

We can usually see the writing on the wall. In plain script, we can see if the problem belongs on our plate or not. If not, then we need to bow out of becoming involved.

****

When each day is the same as the next,
it's because people fail to recognize
the good things that happen in their
lives every day that the sun rises.

--The Alchemist

****

There are times when skirmishes are not at all concerning us. For example, two of your neighbors are in a verbal battle over a fallen tree lying on both properties, and it needs to be removed. There is no clear indication to which property the tree belongs, so who should pay? And on a beautiful, sunny day, while you are watering your gorgeous red roses, both neighbors spot you—and suddenly you become the innocent target. And here they come. What do you do? You know that you are about to get caught in the middle of a situation that isn't yours. Whose problem is it? Not yours, for sure.

****

I don't really care whether my
glass is half full or half empty...I'm
just happy to have a glass.

--Joe Farrel

****

If you allow yourself to become involved in deciding which neighbor should be responsible, you have stepped directly into a bad, stinky situation. The irony of it is that sometimes the two neighbors end up being best of friends, and you are odd person-out with both.

Almost all situations in our lives boil down to a simple question: *"Is this problem mine or someone else's?"* We are not responsible for solving conflicts that clearly belong to the other person. Solving problems for other folks can end up as a disaster just waiting to happen. In order to solve the problems of someone else, we would need to become omniscient. We would have to know the absolute, total truth, beyond any doubts involving the situation.

It is God who knoweth the heart—Luke 16:15

One would think that we would know better than to become involved in a situation that lies on the doorstep of someone else. Whose problem is it? For whatever reason, we may enjoy the power and attention of the involvement, and indeed we get plenty of both. We ride high in the saddle when directing others into what we think is a bright, sunny solution. It may not occur to us that we are possibly getting in God's way of teaching life lessons to that person with the problem.

Problems emerge from our interfering in the life of another human without being asked. Or we may assume that we have fantastic answers to the problems. We enter into another person's territory that solely belongs to God and to the person with the problem. God has a specific plan for that person, and He is perfectly capable of assisting the person without our help. Secondly, there is the danger of the situation backfiring. What happens when our advice backfires in our friend's life? *"Hello, Houston, we have a problem!"* In our hands we now have an outraged friend, in addition to the actual backfiring of the problem. All of this can escalate beyond our craziest imagination.

Thirdly, when we set ourselves up as demigods, we can actually believe in our pseudo-deity. We become an island unto ourselves. And a train wreck is going to occur. We have ceased asking ourselves, *"Whose problem is it?"*

We go into another person's personal arena where the holy angels fear to wander. We have assumed the job of God, without even knowing His plan for the other person. We may end up botching the entire thing because we failed to ask, *"Is this my problem or not?"* Because of our interference, we have wandered into God's plan for the other person—talk about dangerous! Wow! We were never meant to be "small gods" in our neighborhood, family, and community.

Lastly, we set ourselves up to fail. When we take on problems that are not ours, our friend can be left depressed, discouraged, disappointed, and angry because we have steered the person in the wrong direction. A horrendous happening can occur: our friend can end up in worst circumstances. We fail by not realizing that our solution to a problem does not mean it will work in the life of the other person. Misery and disappointment are twin emotions that can hit our friend head-on. As a result, our friend remains confused, and the problem still exists.

"Deciding whose problem is it" will absolutely free you. You no longer have to assume that you must straighten out your entire world of relationships. You will breathe easier by knowing that God is still in control and can help individuals plow through their own fields. Your conscience remains clear and secure because you have not steered someone in the wrong direction.

**Don't get me wrong on this Life Skill. There will be times when you do have to get involved in situations not belonging to you, such as abuse, death and dying, grief, addiction. But be very cautious! We need to tiptoe through these issues.

Not using this No-Nonsense Life Skill can be classified as potentially destructive. For whatever reasons, we humans can trap ourselves in conflicts that are not even remotely close to our affairs. We wake up one morning to find ourselves slap-dab in the midst of problems that wholeheartedly belong on the back steps of others. We may choose to get tangled in the web of their problems because we are searching for excitement in our dreary lives, for superiority over our relationships, or for our personal loneliness.

Moreover, there are folks who end up in the middle of two opposing forces without the foggiest idea of how they became involved. No hint, no clue, no desire. Yet, there they are in the O.K. Corral, verbal guns blasting, with Wyatt Earp Complainer #1 against Frank McLaury, Complainer #2. And as an innocent bystander, we just happen to drive up in our twenty-year old Fiat that we've named Trigger.

If we had been watching and thinking clearly, we would have seen the "gunfight" enactment and established a ten mile berth, with Trigger gunning our trusty Fiat. But perhaps we permitted our curiosity or nosiness to valiantly steer us into that O. K. Corral. Here comes the bloodshed!

I am by no means making light of such a situation, but as a reader with a keen sense of humor, you can laugh or smile because probably you have placed yourself in such an intense, excruciatingly predicament at least once during your lifetime.

Because we may have gotten caught up at that moment in the "verbal gunfight" in the O. K. Corral, we perhaps neglected or just plain forgot to ask ourselves the question: *"Whose problem is it? Mine or theirs? If the obvious answer is theirs, how come I'm getting in the middle?"* This Life Skill may seem heartless, detached, and uncaring because we are choosing to stay out of the traffic. On the other hand, if we decide to continually become involved in problems that are not ours, we need to wear our "six shooters" because we most likely will always find ourselves in a never-ending battle.

Not all therapy situations are gloom and doom. Some can actually be fun, even humorous. Carrie and Crystal were identical twins of fourteen. Their parents referred them to me after each parent claimed being driven to the "loony bin" by their daughters having constant babbling disagreements. I was instructed by the parents either to "fix" the situation or to dismiss the two girls and to enroll the parents in therapy sessions.

My first impression of the twins was their hysterical sense of humor. They would feed off of one another, and I couldn't help but get tickled.

A misconception of therapy is that a person must be in dire straits in order to seek help. Many of my clients are in therapy so that they can keep a healthy equilibrium on a daily basis. With the insurmountable stress, expectations, and mundane responsibilities that each of us faces from one day to the next, having an objective person in our arena can greatly help. It can be refreshing to have a professional in our lives who will be clear-minded and knowledgeable, and even with a sense of humor. The case with Crystal and Carrie was that they did not need therapy but did benefit from the experience.

The twins were charming and delightful. When some issues became aggravating to them, their humor became priceless. Their issues were simple. Each had not yet learned to mind her own particular affairs and to refrain from involving herself with the issues of the other sister. Cassie believed that she was totally responsible to take Crystal's problems as if they were hers, and vice-versa. Because their daily problems became such a hodgepodge, solving issues for the other sister produced hurt feelings, distress, and anxiety. Each girl was assuming that the problems belonging to the other was hers to solve. It became a disaster!

Being joined at the hip was an understatement. Cassie and Crystal were not free to deal effectively with their own personal issues without the well-meaning interference from the other. It looked much like a circus of performers who were all over the place, in one another's lives, trying to reach solutions to conflicts that belonged to the other. In addition, at times the twins would try to wander into the issues facing their parents. Two fourteen year-olds who believed, in a non-confrontal way, that they were fully capable of solving adult issues.

At times, if it had not been comical from the viewpoints of these beautifully-acting twins, I probably would have had to see a therapist at the end of their sessions.

Once again, the emphasis is to know whose problem is it that you are wanting to solve. If you are dealing with issues that belong to someone else in which that person is fully qualified to face, solve, and move on, then back away.

Here are some questions we need to ask ourselves if we are butting in where angels fear to go:

1. Are we unknowingly interfering with God's Plan to deal spiritually with the individual having the conflict?
2. Do we sincerely want to be in the middle of God's intentions?
3. Have we really, really prayed about entering into the conflict?

4. Are we willing to run the risk of having God deal with us due to our interference (and believe me, He will)?

5. What is the absolute truth for the reason of my being in the middle of the conflict? Be completely honest with yourself.

You have a choice. You can absolutely **STOP** moseying into the Corral of others, thus causing a stampede. It's entirely your mature choice.

Stand

Tall

On

Principles

You can change your life with just one choice.

Suggestions: *Even when invited into the space of another, seek the Lord's insights and pure, Divine guidance.*

Stay closely in touch with your own feelings and thoughts to know what to say and to know when to stop.

Think, think, think before you give your advice to people.

Always ask yourself the question: "Is this my problem or not?"

P.S. To all my friends whom I gave advice to when we were teenagers, I hereby apologize. I was young and inexperienced as young people usually are about Life Skills. I didn't have the sense to keep my mouth shut and point you to a qualified adult to get help. Again, I apologize.

Your next stop may at times be heart-breaking, but it must be done if you are going to grow spiritually and emotionally.

CHAPTER 11

NO NONSENSE DEPARTURE

Be the best you can, and stop wishing you were different. Follow your heart, cherish the gifts that make you special, respect yourself, and people will respect you. Surround yourself with good people.

--Christopher Gaida

Dedicated to the loving supporters of the Youth Program at Northeast Park Baptist Church

CHAPTER 11

Many people come and go during our lifetime. If we tried to count the number, it would easily be in the thousands. Childhood pals, elementary, middle, high school friends, college comrades, career associates, church folks, volunteers, family members, and civic club members all have combined to help us become the individuals we are. Even with our current remarkable wireless communication system, it would be quite impossible to maintain contact with the endless number of people.

It is obvious that we have to let go of people as we move from one life stage to another. We barely can keep up with people in our immediate circle. We claim everyone as our friends. And yet researchers claim that during our life on earth, we will have truthfully only one genuine, true friend—a person who knows **all** of our strengths and weaknesses, past and present bad and good experiences, and still loves us. If we have two life friends, then we are greatly blessed. If we have three, then we are the exception. Four friends? Hum-m-m-m-m. Really? Name them. We would like to believe that we have a multiplicity of true friends. It feeds our delicious ego. So for argument sake, we will pretend that all the multitude of people we know are our genuine friends.

The No-Nonsense of this Life Style is the necessity to weed out carefully those individuals in our lives who are destructive. They do not add one positive element into our relationship. They can take a sunny day of ours and turn it quickly into a dismal and boring experience. They are like a dark cloud hovering over us, and any umbrella of hope of ours to survive in the relationship is emotionally choking. We attempt to battle their onslaught of negativity and pessimistic attitudes, but inside we know that we are losing in the battle of the minds. After a visit with them, we are emotionally and physically exhausted All of us have these types of people in our lives.

Because these individuals can be like parasites in our lives, there is a necessity to move them out of our lives if we are planning on surviving. Giving them departure papers will probably be one of the most difficult things for you to do. Letting go is quite like cleaning out one's attic or garage. There are those places in our homes that are filled with unsightly clutter, and when we clean out the clutter, we feel better. We feel in control. We feel happier. Some individuals in our arena represent our messy attic or garage. They clutter up our minds with negativity. They build their happiness on our unhappiness, and they have no redeeming quality that can add to our lives, only take away. We spend so much time with them that we miss out on being with those who add precious moments to our lives.

****

Your life is a continuous portrait,
Painted more colorful every day
From the brush strokes of the people
You meet along the way.

--Linda Ellis

****

It isn't simple to let people go, especially if we have known them for a long time. We feel uneasy and awkward. One of the discomforts is actually doing it. We have no clue how they will respond. They may feel hurt, angry, sad, and disappointment. And at that moment we may not exactly feel joyous. And yet, we know it must be done if we want to be a complete, contented, positive self.

Other feelings regarding the departure process may be fear and worry. What will be the repercussions? Will the repercussions be severe? We just don't know. Are we sure that we are doing the right thing? Questions, questions, decisions, decisions. *"God, please help me."*

We have to remember that God is not taken by surprise regarding this dilemma of ours. So while we are getting bent way out of proportion about the dismissal of certain individuals in our lives, God is way ahead of us. He is not going to leave us without friends—those individuals who will make our life a blessing, an adventure, and lots of fun. There are friends in your life right now who will remain there by your side. Those folks are the real friends!

Kelly was an attractive lady in her mid-forties. Her personality was equally the same as her exquisite beauty. She could stop traffic for miles by jaywalking across the street. Her poise, style, and demeanor served as a magnet that drew people to her. What kept people loyal to her was her unfailing kindness, her genuine interest in others, and her never ending desire to be a trustworthy friend. She seemed to have her act together. It would have certainly been an atomic shock to her friends if they had known she sought out professional counseling. Individuals had placed her on a glorified pedestal that was not tarnished or destructible. Placing her on such a pedestal seemed to them the correct thing to do, and some deemed it an unspeakable honor.

Because of who and what she really felt, being promoted to the pedestal status, was atrocious and highly embarrassing. She had absolutely no desire whatsoever of having all the attention from the folks who found their way into her arena.

Kelly lived a life of people-pleasing. She went places that she didn't want to go. She forced herself to tolerate being with people whom she didn't care to be around. And she volunteered to do things that were not her cup of tea. To be blunt, she was a puppet on a worn-out string, at the mercy of whoever was in charge at the moment.

Kelly had difficulty in saying "No" to others. It was not evident on her exterior, but it was totally a different story on the interior. Little did people know, she was diagnosed with mild to moderate depression, panic attacks, migraines, and a stomach peptic ulcer. She had never learned to be a self-assertive individual, and that led to her difficulty in being a self-actualizing individual. She found it impossible to guide her own life towards her worthwhile goals, to declare to others her intentions with her life, and to demand respect from those who made up her personal arena.

Just because a person has "stop and stare" good looks does not mean that they are cool, calm, and collective on the inside. Whether it be a male or female, a people-pleaser exists like a prisoner, shackled to the demands of others. It is usually a horrible lifestyle.

There were people in Kelly's life whom she wanted out, but she didn't have the nerve or fortitude to make it come to pass. These individuals were too forceful, and Kelly was too timid. These uninvited guests in her world were continually sucking the life out of her well-being. They had Kelly wrapped around their desires and expectations. Going particular places that they deemed necessary, doing whatever they wished, and being with individuals they selected day-in and day-out was the only lifestyle that Kelly really knew. And she had been doing this behavior for so long that it had become her comfort zone. She had accepted her physical and mental conditions as being normal. She didn't have the self-confidence or self-esteem or know-how to put an end to her people-pleasing personality. So, year after year, she suffered, and she ultimately became worse.

On the advice of her physician, she decided to seek professional counseling. To get a clear image of Kelly's dilemma, picture a cluster of grapes. Each grape represented a conflict in Kelly's life: depression, panic attacks, sadness, exhaustion, migraines, ulcer, frustration, lack of self-esteem. Some individuals enter therapy with only one of those specific concerns, but not so with Kelly. She had all of them., bombarding her every day. She represented a dart board, and wherever the dart landed on the board on any given day, she had to try keeping her head above water. Her therapeutic journey was wide open for exploration.

My idea was to begin with teaching Kelly self-assertive techniques. We both agreed that she had individuals in her environment who needed to be escorted out. These particular people were not contributing to her life but rather devouring it, day by day. They had to go. This indeed would be very difficult for Kelly to do when the time arrived. It would go against her nature, and doing so would take her out of her comfort zone. Because Kelly had multiple diagnostic problems, the sessions were intense and at times heart-breaking.

At one time or the other, all of us have had individuals in our lives who were liabilities. They added absolutely nothing to our well-being. When we needed someone to lean on, they were too busy. When we needed to be uplifted, they were critical. When we needed to vent our feelings, they were judgmental. Some of us may still have people in our arena who suck out our enthusiasm, confidence, and positive attitude. Perhaps like Kelly, we have not reached the point of weeding out those folks. We remain at their mercy. We exist in a very sad, frustrating, and gloomy world.

As the days turned into months, Kelly tried sincerely to improve her life. We discussed what needed to be done. Furthermore, she had no trouble naming the individuals who were the negative forces in her life. There were weeks in therapy when Kelly made leaps and bounds towards discovering her new self. During that time, her self-esteem became a beacon in her dark, forlorn world.

And then there were times when Kelly's advancement was minimum, if at all. Her people-pleasing facade became foremost in her daily, routine life. She became a victim of the very people who continued to stampede on her self-surviving parade. As a result, her depression worsened, and the panic attacks increased. It was sad to watch her self-image suffocate due to her need to please people. At times she was like a small child reaching out to be held by someone who cared, but not receiving it. There were days when Kelly became desperate—to be stronger, happier, freer. Kelly wanted to make advancements, but her people-pleasing need was much stronger— too powerful, too awesome.

While she will not dissolve from such a personal need of freedom, Kelly will die inside many times throughout a normal day's activities, surrounded by individuals who demand her attention. This account of Kelly has a sad ending. She gave up on herself due to desperation and intense frustration. Perhaps the need and expected changes did not occur fast enough in her mind. Kelly just quit attending her therapy sessions. No calls from her, thus no explanations, no return calls, no nothing.

On the exterior, Kelly will maintain her gorgeous appearance. Kelly will more than likely continue to be the subject of ill treatment by some of her negative acquaintances who have established homestead rights within her arena. And Kelly will maintain her people-pleasing personality trait, as her depression deepens and her panic attacks occur more frequently. Her exterior may appear in fine shape, but her internal self is like an accident on the interstate just ready to happen.

You and I have the inalienable right to select the individuals who add to our lives, and also that right includes dismissing those who are self-serving, harshly critical, mean-spirited, and everlastingly a royal disaster. We can **Stop** our never-ending misery by dismissing those who cause our drinking glass to be half-empty rather than completely full.

Stand
Tall
On
Principles

Suggestions: *Before dismissing specific people in your life, pray about your decision.*
Pray for those whom you know must be dismissed.
Write a letter to those persons to explain why you are dismissing them, but DO NOT SEND IT. This suggestion is strictly a therapeutic assignment for you.
Thank the Lord for giving you the confidence to part with certain people.
Don't allow yourself to feel guilty about your decision.

*It was my luck to have a few good teachers
in my youth, men and women, who came
into my dark head and lit a match.*

--*Yann Martel*

**All of us use hurtful and damaging words
in our everyday conversations. The next
chapter tells you which ones they are.**

CHAPTER 12

NO-NONSENSE WORD USAGE

Be careful of the words you say
To keep them soft and sweet
You never know from day to day,
Which ones you'll have to eat.

--author unknown

Dedicated to Opal Young,
Piper Taylor, and Jada Taylor for
their help with the front cover.

CHAPTER 12

NO-NONSENSE WORD USAGE

There are five words that we freely use in our everyday conversations that can be disastrous and hurtful: **What If, Should, Ought, But, and Why**. In more conversations than not, these words can present a distorted image to the listener and to ourselves. And yet, they are five of our commonly used communication words. They can be correctly used in everyday conversations, however, they can also be used to sling guilt (**should, ought**), to question another person's judgment (**but, why**), or to create doubt and worry **(what if)**.

"Should" and "Ought" are words that can cause a simple, innocent conversation turn ugly in a heartbeat. They imply that a person "should" be behaving, or not, in a specific way. *"You should be paying more attention to your neighbors," "You ought to be reading more books,"* or *"You shouldn't be acting so silly."* The exact same message is sent with "Ought"--to do or not to do some particular action. *"You ought to be ashamed of yourself"* or *"He ought to work harder than he is."* These statements are aimed at creating feelings of guilt and despair. What is taking place is that individuals are taking their own standards within their belief system to evaluate and to judge another person's behavior. Thus, it is another person's standards that are being used to promote their thinking, their value system, their ideas of how we "Should" and "Ought" to behave and to believe. In a conversation in which an individual begins using "Should" and "Ought" our invisible "red flag" needs to shoot straight up and to sound an alarm. That person's value system has entered into the conversation with us possibly in mind. If the usage of "Should" and "Ought" occurs, we have to remember that their belief system came from **their** parents, grandparents, relatives, friends, or bosses, but necessarily not from ours. Furthermore, we have to be extremely careful that we don't question or evaluate our personal value system according to the standards of another person. Since we don't have the same historical background, our belief system may differ with their standards.

Whenever we are communicating with someone else, we would do well to avoid using "Should" and "Ought"--it will safeguard the conversation. Each person has a value system that strictly belongs to that individual.

There are times when each one of us needs to examine one's own value system to determine if we truly adhere to each standard that we were given at a young age. We may have to let go of standards that we truthfully don't agree with any longer. If you were told as a child that going to a Sunday movie or playing cards might be wrong, do you still believe such? The issue is that each one of us must develop our own personal belief system which means analyzing and evaluating what we truthfully believe as our personal standards and **not** those of someone else.

****

A timely word may lessen stress, but a loving word may heal and bless.

****

We communicate particular words in our conversations that have the potential of creating havoc with those whom we are speaking. We are so accustomed in using them that we may not be conscious of the damage that they can create. Two of such words are "But" and "Why"--these words can boldly trample across a person's self-esteem. They are like a double-edged sword—we can be on the receiving end as well as on the giving end. These two words have the potential of making a person doubt one's capability of reaching effective solutions to everyday problems.

****

Many a blunt word has a sharp edge.

--Unknown

****

Whenever we are asked a question with "Why" we immediately put up our defense wall: *"Why did you say that?" "Why are you doing that?" "Why don't you tell me the truth?"* Our defense wall dates back to when at an early age, we were always being asked "Why"— and in order to justify our behavior, we had to come up with a good reason, at least what we thought was a good answer. Parents, teachers, and whoever else had authority over us at the time demanded an answer. The word "Why" came to be a mental exercise of satisfying the person asking us. There were times when we didn't have the foggiest idea of the reason behind our actions, but we needed to get the "heat" off of us. At the time of the question-answer session, we knew we had to at least provide a half decent response to the "Why" question. To save face, we gave whatever excuse we could muster up.

Because memories of the "Why" days are firmly cemented into our subconscious mind, we react defensively when the word "Why" begins a question: *"Why are you late for work?"* *"Why are you always watching football games?"* The "Why" triggers our memories of yesteryear. And ironically, we find ourselves starting conversations with "Why" and expecting an answer--the very word that we detest, we aim it at others. Irony at its best.

Rather than asking a "Why" question, there are two non-threatening words--**"How come"** and **"What"**--*"How come you reacted the way you did?"* *"How come you forgot my birthday?"* *"What was your reason for misbehaving?"* The words "How come" and "What" do not usually erect a mental and emotional barrier. And as a result, we are likely to receive truthful answers, plus having a pleasant conversation.

****

> ### *Try to use small words.*
> ### *It is hard to do, but they say*
> ### *what you mean.*
> ### *If you don't know what you mean,*
> ### *use big words,*
> ### *They will confuse the people.*
>
> #### *--Author unknown*

****

We feel less stressful in our lines of communication when appropriate words are used. In the English language, the word "But" is used to connect thoughts: *"The sun is out, but a storm is heading this way."* There is absolutely nothing wrong with the usage of "But" in a sentence. In fact, it is required in some communications. However, it can be used as a demeaning three-letter word. It can undo the quintessence of a genuine compliment: *"She is such a sweet girl, but her people skills are lacking,"* or *"He is a very handsome person, but he doesn't know how to groom himself very well."* Because we have a tendency at times to focus on the negative aspects in life, our attention is drawn to the words after the "But" – the power of negativity can be overwhelming. We hear the part of the girl being a sweet girl, but we tend to place our main attention on her weakness of lacking people skills or the boy not knowing how to groom himself.

There are reasons we place a negative in a positive statement. Perhaps we are jealous of the individual's attributes, and we counteract the positive in order to place ourselves on a higher status level. By insulting the person, we feed our ego needs. Another reason for a "put-down" is to gain undivided attention from others. Ever notice how much attention a person receives when one has some juicy gossip to share? Thus, the easy way to receive the attention is to use a "But" in a condemning way. People will come a-running to hear what we have to say. We start a statement with a positive (sweet girl) in order to give the impression that we mean well. Then we slide in the negative (people skills). It appears that we are thinking of the very best about a person, and then comes the "But" word.

For whatever reasons we use a negative after a positive with a "But" we need to remember that what goes around comes around... eventually.

Our shock and hurt will come when we are on the receiving end-- *"You are the sharpest person I've ever met, BUT you use much too much lipstick." "You have so many friends, BUT maybe it's because of the money you have."* What a jolt to a person's self-esteem! We certainly were not prepared for that grenade in our foxhole.

Whenever you and I make use of the word "But" to hurt someone, to damage a person's self-esteem, or to promote oneself above the other person, then we are playing a destructive game. People are going to suffer, and feelings are going to be damaged. We are being derogatory and mean-spirited. Eventually our behavior will result in our existing in a stressful and harsh reality. The tables will turn—against us. And such stress can undo us. If we continue playing such a destructive game, at the expense of others, then our lives will be nothing more than stress, stress, and more stress. It can become totally out of control due to our own negativity and of our need to be the "top dog" in the crowd.

Suggestions: *When you catch yourself using the two words of "Should" and "Ought" then stop. Rewind. Start the sentence over again.*

Attempt not using "Why" in your conversations. When you notice using it, stop and re-word the statement with "How come" or "What"--

If you are using "But" in your conversations, use it correctly.

It is never meant to be a put-down on someone else. Make a fun game out of not using "But"--ask your friends to catch you when you are using it in a negative put-down.

The reward for them is a dollar each time. Believe me, you will quickly get rid of the negative "But" in your conversations.

Practice not using "Should" and "Ought" until it becomes a healthy habit.

If there were ever a word combination in the English language that can cause severe repercussions, it would be "**What if**"--this word combination can be horrific.

There is a "What if" that is harmless and actually beneficial. The "What if" that has accompanied experiments has led to many wonderful discoveries. *"It didn't work that way correctly. What if we attempt it this way?" "What if we use another brand instead of what we've been using?"*

However, the "What if" that can completely immobilize our present objectives, desires, future plans and goals can have pessimism, depression, and confusion as its bedfellows. *"What if I fail the class?" "What if there is no need for my help in five years?" "What if I get too old to drive?"*

Our present and future plans can be annihilated when the "What if" doubts creep into our minds, and the stress we place upon ourselves can be mind-boggling. When the "What if" becomes part of our thinking, we end up with a horrible and threatening case of the "What if" syndrome. Our minds, with the "What if" attitude, can trick us into actually believing all of our "What if" situations. *"What if I move overseas and a deadly disease hits the small community where I'll be staying?" "What if I go to the beach and get really sunburned?" "What if no one reads this book entitled No-Nonsense Life Skills?"* Our "What if" thought processing can stop us dead in our tracks. As a result, we spend an unbelievable amount of time recoiling, rebounding, and reflecting over what actions or events might happen in our lives.

The "What if" thinking process starts in our minds when the very first small doubt enters. Rather than immediately dismissing it, we begin feeding it with additional "What if" thinking. *"What if nobody picks me up at the airport?" "What if my friend forgets to take care of my pets while I'm on vacation?"*

When the "What if" thinking becomes more powerful than our logical, rational thinking, we have lost the battle. The "What if" thinking has won. Sadly, we've become our own worst victim because at that point, no one can always plow through the "What if" doubts and fears. We have enclosed ourselves into an invisible mental and emotional cage of our own doing.

****

The oldest, shortest words--"yes" and "no"-- are those which require the most thought.

--Pythagoras

****

There can be times when we can outwit the message that we are receiving from our skeptical "What if" thinking. We are able to follow through with our plans, without the doubts. However, we must be careful of potential ambushes from well-intended family members and friends. They are not necessarily trying to sabotage our present goals and future plans. They may be overprotective, and therefore, they introduce doubts into our minds—and we are saddled into their "What if" questions. *"What if you run out of money while on vacation?"* *"What if your migraines start up again?"* These individuals, without meaning to do it, can place uncertainties in our plans. More times than not, they are well-meaning people but way over the limit of being too protective. They are called "helicopter friends."

When we have reached a decision regarding our plans and goals, we naturally want to share it with those whom we love. The conversation may be going great until....

Without warning, a verbal grenade is thrown into our sandbox. Boom! The "What if" questions come from all sides: *"What if you lose your way?"* *What if you get sick?"* *"What if everything goes wrong?"* We find ourselves being "What if"-to-death. Our answers to their questions can't come fast enough to satisfy the concerns of everyone. While we are trying to provide answers, more and more "What if" questions are coming so quick that our frustration and stress limits are steadily climbing. Since unresolved frustration leads to anger, that is exactly what begins to happen within us. What was to be a happy, spirit-lifting meeting turns into a monumental disaster. Feelings are damaged. And we feel dismayed by all of the "What if" questions. Our plans seem to be headed for the mental dumpster, and we are left to retrieve our plans from that dumpster because the dump truck is a-coming.

You and I have a choice of existing in a "What if" cage or of living life to its fullest, even with involved risks. "What if" individuals are always second guessing themselves while existing in their stressful, confused state of mind. They drive themselves daily to the loony bin, while also including on the trip their family and friends.

As long as our risks are not destructive, hurtful, or dangerous, dump the "What if" existence and enjoy living to your fullest every single day. Some of the risks will backfire. So what if they do? After you recover, the mountains will still be majestic, the streams will still be flowing, and a full moon will still remain awesome-looking.

****

Success is never final, failure is never fatal.

--*John Wooden*

****

It is far better that we live our lives with healthy risks than living in a "What if" cage that we have constructed out of doubts and fears. The only person who can keep us prisoners in that cage is ourselves. No one else has that power unless we have given it to them.

> *"I have come that you may have life, and that you*
> *may have it more abundantly. (John 10:10)*

You and I cannot possibly have the abundant life that God has promised if we are living in the shadow of the "What if" circumstances. It all depends on one person—You.

Suggestions: *Begin now to eliminate your "What if" thinking.*
Catch yourself when you are giving in to a "What if" process of thinking.
Be extra careful of associating often with "What if" people. They have a tendency to bring us down to their way of "cage thinking."
Purchase a positive-oriented devotional book and read it faithfully each day.
Stay positive. Don't dwell on the negatives in your life.
Be brave to take healthy risks.
At the end of the day, ask yourself if you really "lived" fully or just plain existed.
Enjoy your life and those in your arena by doing fun Activities on a regular basis.

Remember: This life is not a dress rehearsal.
Enjoy, Enjoy your life.

**The upcoming chapter will be the most
difficult No-Nonsense Life Skill to master.**

CHAPTER 13

NO-NONSENSE SELF EXPECTATIONS

Expectations: an invitation to resentments.

--unknown

Dedicated to Gail Barcus, Rene Burton, and Cecil Yates who do not place any expectations on me.

CHAPTER 13

NO-NONSENSE SELF EXPECTATIONS

Of all the Life Skills, one of the most difficult ones, if not the hardest, to master is that of expectations. It becomes a valid and workable Life Skill **only** when we can reach that point of expecting nothing from others—absolutely nothing...no expectations. The reason it is the hardest No-Nonsense Life Skill to accomplish dates back to when we were children. We were expected to do certain tasks and to carry out particular responsibilities. Failure to do so meant having to deal with our parents. Being successful in carrying them out meant praise and possible rewards. Thus, expectations have a history of longevity.

The very idea of having no expectations is massive in our mind-set, and so very difficult to actually apply in our relationships and in our daily life. Remember the many times we were given a promise by a friend or family member, and it didn't happen? Remember the sadness we felt, and perhaps the anger and frustration we experienced when the promise was not honored? Why did it bother us so much?

It is natural to have expectations. After all, we have grown up with the idea that people should keep their word. We place our trust in their integrity to do as they say. If someone tells us that a certain thing will be done, then we expect it to be carried out. Should be simple, right? But not so. When the promise doesn't take place, our hearts are broken, our hopes dashed, and our expectations mutilated.

All of us at one time or the other have not lived up to our promises. We failed to be where we said, we didn't complete the work we promised, other circumstances kept us from doing what we gave our word on—all of these represent broken promises which resulted in someone's expectations not being met. We have all done it.

What takes place in the minds and lives of the people who expect someone to do what is promised? As kids and teenagers, we filled our heads with the places we wanted to visit, the food we wanted to order, and the activities we planned to do. We waited patiently by the door with the hopes that the doorbell would soon ring by that special person who was going to whisk us away. Or, as adults, we plan our day around that particular person coming to repair some needed service to our home. Or, maybe if all goes well we plan to attend a movie with a friend or to shop the mall. We are expecting that individual to be present as promised. When no one shows up, we are left to process our thoughts and feelings of disappointment and frustration.

It is hard not to judge those who failed to keep their promise, especially when we are the ones who received the hurt. The disappointment can be painful. Our expectations seemed fair to us. We were expecting for someone to do what they said.

What problems follow expectations? With each expectation, we set up ourselves possibly to be hurt, disappointed, sadden, deflated. Springing up in us can be a garden variety of raw emotions: anger, guilt, bitterness, resentment, revenge, and frustration. As certain as the sun appears in the morning, so will our negative feelings towards those who do not fulfill our expectations. Having expectations of others creates unbelievable stress in one's life. Our expectations become dangerous when we are hoping that someone will fulfill our lives, make us happier, make us successful.

****

Expectations are fragile and easily shattered.

--Dean Koontz

****

We have placed our expectations, our hopes, and our happiness in the hands of another individual. When that person fails to meet our expectations, then we can easily feel neglected, abused, violated. Our time, energy, and belief in others have been damaged because another human being did not meet our expectations.

What happens when we continue to place expectations on others? When those individuals finally do have the time and energy to satisfy our expectations successfully, then we turn around and raise our expectations to a higher level on those persons. Higher and higher we go. In every instance, once our expectations are accomplished, our human nature does what it does best—creates more expectations for those individuals. We may even ignore what a person has already done for us. Our focus, unfortunately, is on what the individual hasn't done or on what else we want the person to do. Eventually, those people, through their struggles to fulfill our expectations, can no longer hope to meet them. Finally, the individuals throw up their hands in defeat. And as a result, those of us with the expectations no longer can have our "wants" honored and reached. Thus, we have set ourselves up for failure--to be hurt and disappointed. It becomes a vicious cycle.

****

I finally found a place where the grass is greener on the other side, but now I'm too old to climb the fence.

--Unknown

****

The question that I am usually asked is, *"Don't I have the right to expect my partner to do specific things in our relationship?"* The answer is NO, NO, NO. (Very few people like my response.) It is correct that each person in a relationship has responsibilities in order to keep the relationship functioning properly, whether it be with friends or family. However, if the responsibilities become "expectations"-- then the result can become chaotic. Our expectations may be too demanding, too overwhelming—and the result may be fusses, fights, disagreements—no matter what we actually call it, the scene becomes a disaster.

Then the response I usually get is, *"I'll end up doing everything in the relationship if I end the expectations and trust the responsibility side."* When that happens, a meeting of the minds and emotions needs to occur. If that doesn't produce positive results, bring in a third, objective person to referee. If nothing seems to work to get that person to be responsible, then go ahead and do the responsibilities yourself--if you plan to remain in the relationship. Yes, yourself! It'll be far better in the long run than hoping your expectations will become a reality. **Warning**: if you are saddled in carrying out all the responsibilities, you need to be on guard that bitterness, anger, and resentment does not homestead in your psyche because they surely will try.

Warning to those who are not carrying their own weight in a relationship: Don't think for one little moment that the responsible one will continue doing what you don't. Relationships like those die on the vine. Healthy relationships demand more than just one person doing the "maintenance" work. All types of relationships must have a balance, and the balance requires responsibilities on each person.... but not expectations!

Let me repeat: this No-Nonsense Life Skill is one of the most difficult to master. It may take days, months, and perhaps years to incorporate this Life Skill into your everyday lifestyle. It may become a day-by-day challenge. Expectations continue to creep in, unannounced, unwanted, and certainly unbelievable at times. Whether we are waiting on a phone call, sitting in a doctor's office, hurrying through traffic, needing our vehicle serviced, we must acknowledge the challenge of having no expectations—at times we will succeed and at other times, we will fail. We cannot measure expectations by how small, large, important, or crucial they might be. Expectations are expectations!

If there was ever a client of mine who made me want to seek out a fellow therapist for my own sake, it was Joshua. Joshua was in his late fifties, married, two children of grown age, and successful in his private business. From the beginning of our sessions, it was apparent that he was restless, fidgety, and unhappy for being in therapy. He was in counseling as an order from his wife--*"Either you get counseling or I'm leaving you."* From the very get-go, this would not be "therapy at its best." A person forced into counseling sessions is a challenge equal to crossing Niagara Falls on a tightrope with no safety harness.

Because his wife chose not to accompany him on the first visit, the first few sessions were hunt-and-peck. We hit upon many topics that might have caused his visits, but none of them was on target. It was like searching for that needle planted in the therapeutic haystack. Search, search, search.

It turned out that Joshua had a personal need, almost compulsion, to control the comings and goings of his family members to the point that they avoided him at all cost. However, Joshua was the family patriarch, and he was unaccustomed to being challenged by his family or his associates. It wasn't any wonder that his associates harbored hostility, frustration, anger, and resentment.

In addition to being the controller of his family members, his obsessions spilled out into his professional business. He was not comfortable in assigning responsibilities to his employees and then letting go. Joshua felt compelled to watch over their work, evaluate it on the spot, and verbally demand that the completed job be done to his exact specifications. As one can expect, his employees developed severe stressful ailments to the point that absenteeism in Joshua's company reached a mammoth percentage. And not everyone was playing hooky. They were actually physically ill.

Joshua believed that since he was defraying the therapeutic cost, he had the right to control the therapy sessions. Furthermore, he had unrealistic "expectations" from his therapeutic journey. Total havoc became a part of his journey, and the journey did not go far or last long.

Since Joshua was accustomed to being in charge of the lives of those in his arena, naturally he expected those individuals to fall dutifully in line. In his mind-set, one simply does not question the orders of a high commander, and there was no doubt that he considered himself as the commander.

Since his behavioral conduct was satisfied by his narcissistic desires and beliefs, Joshua introduced his "have it my way" demeanor into his therapy sessions, little by little. Warning! Do not enter the "sacred doors" of a professional therapist with even the remote belief that you are in charge of the sessions and that the therapist is there for the exhilarating ride.

While the therapeutic relationship never developed into an one-upmanship, it never had the opportunity to gain momentum. Bona fide "therapeutic traveling" has only one steam captain, and it's not the client. He is a paying, privileged passenger on the journey. No debate. No compromise. No alternatives.

Sadly, Joshua's steamboat therapeutic tour was short. He was not willing or perhaps able to relinquish his controls, verbal demands, and unrealistic expectations. He departed as he arrived—a controlling, domineering individual who, unlike Huck Finn, wasn't free to enjoy his "steamboat" escapade. I have no idea whether his marriage survived the turmoil, or if his children tolerated the continuous abuse, or whether his associates believed their salaries were worth the stress.

You and I can **STOP** having expectations toward others in our arena. However, it will require the super strength of Superman, the delicate finesse of Snow White, the sheer determination of Cinderella, and the enduring patience of Job.

Stand

Tall

On

Principles

Extraordinary people do the ordinary things extraordinarily well even when doing them ordinary is good enough.

--Coach Rick Robinson

Suggestions: *Be continually aware to identify expectations when they occur.*

Before expectations become unmanageable, talk out the expectations with a neutral party

Don't beat yourself up when you are guilty of expectations.

Try to use humor when your expectations are in control.

Keep expectations from escalating by staying vigilant.

When your expectations interfere with relationships, be wise and honorable to apologize and make things right.

Remember:

Don't give up on these Life Skills. Every single day can be an exciting challenge. You have the choice!

Two uplifting challenges:

Challenge #1
"Anytime you devalue people, you question God's creation of them. You can never tell people too often, too loudly, or too publicly how much you love them."

---John C. Maxwell

Challenge #2
"Life's challenges are not supposed to paralyze you, they're supposed to help you discover who you are."

--Bernice Johnson Reagon

LAST COMMENTS

If you have made it to the end of this book without throwing it out, using it to start your fireplace, or giving up on the No-Nonsense Life Skills, then congratulations! You have the opportunity to live an abundant life— worthwhile thoughts, healthy feelings, and ethical actions. These Life Skills are not the easiest to apply to one's everyday life due to our many distractions. Plus, these Skills are very challenging. They are not for the weak because the weak will not use them—they will give up.

Each one of us has the ability, capacity, and opportunity to be content and thriving. We cannot pretend to understand everything in our world, but we can be understanding people towards those who are less privileged, neglected, forgotten, and downtrodden. (Gary Pennell) If we are to offer genuine understanding to others, then we need to know ourselves and to how we function. Thus, the purpose of this book. It cannot solve all problems, and it doesn't intend to do so. However, its principles can enable you to have a wonderful, exciting, spiritual journey. I am proof of that...in a humble way!

I would enjoy hearing about your journey. You can e-mail me at the following address:

therainmaker345@gmail.com
or
my web page
rayashurst.com
My promise to you will be a response.

FOOTNOTES

Doan, Eleanor. <u>Sourcebook for Speakers</u>. Zondervan, 1968.

Ellis, Linda. <u>Live Your Dash</u>. Sterling Ethos, 2011.

Hefley, James C. <u>A Dictionary of Illustrations</u>. Zondervan, 1971.

Hefley, James C. <u>The Sourcebook of Humor</u>. Zondervan, 1968.

Lee, Robert G. <u>Sourcebook of 500 Illustrations</u>. Zondervan, 1964.

Michelini, Michael. "Adventures in Life and Business. Permalink (October 17, 2010)

Scofield, C. I. (ed). <u>The New Scofield Reference Bible</u>. Oxford Press, 1967.

The Next Book

Real Death and Then Life

Dr. Ray Ashurst

**"Your little girl is dying. I'm so sorry.
There's nothing that can be done."**

The conference room became a horrendous nightmare as the mortified parents attempted to grasp what their teary-eyed doctor was saying.

"No! No! No! You're wrong. Do more tests. Do something, please. Please"

But the pleading words from the little girl's Dad was drowned out by the hysterical Mom who had lost control. Grabbing her chair to lend support did not meet her needs as she slowly slid to the polished floor, drawing unto herself her arms and hands, signifying absolute denial.

A single statement that announces the death of a loved one can stop us in our daily tracks. All the things we had scheduled for that day become a blur of responsibilities which no longer are priorities. Our busy agenda stops. Our well-meaning tasks are of no consequence, and our lives as we knew it disappears—permanently. No power on earth has the ability to restore us to what we once deemed normalcy.

Printed in the United States
By Bookmasters